Girl, Just Quit!

Brandy Butler

Girl, Just Quit!

ISBN-13: 978-0692607145

Published by: Brandy Butler Media, LLC.

Book Website - www.brandybutleronline.com
Email - info@brandybutleronline.com

Dedication

Dear Lord,

Thank you for guiding me.

Thank you for protecting me from things seen and unseen.

Thank you for your abundance, grace and beauty.

Thank you for stirring up a flame that I never knew I had.

Thank you loving me ever so gently.

Thank you for your oil of anointing because I know that it is you that has shaped up and formed the greatness that flows inside of me and allows me touch others.

Thank you for divine connections and for your angels that you have sent to help me along the way. I couldn't have done this on my own.

Thank you for expanding my vision and expanding me in the process.

Thank you for the readers and the lives that this book touches.

Most of all, thank you for the process. It has been through my imperfect action, and your sweet, sweet process that I have discovered and committed to my divine calling.

Contents

Acknowledgments

To my husband Barry, thank you for standing with me in my darkest hour and supporting me through the challenges of running a business. I love you.

To my children, Jayden, Jordan, and Kendall, I pray that you three know that everything I do is for you. You three are the reason I wake and breathe and I thank God for entrusting your precious lives to me. May you all grow up knowing that you can be and do whatever your hearts desire.

To my mother, Mildred, you are the reason that I am so strong and have such a strong knack for getting things done no matter what. Thank you for showing me what beauty and strength look like.

To my father, Pervis, thank you for exposing me to the possibilities of wealth at a young age. You are the reason for my untamed entrepreneurial spirit.

To my aunt Ann, thank you for truly being a second mother to me. There is no way that I could have grown my business fulltime without the love and support that you've ALWAYS offered me. I'm forever grateful.

To the world's greatest support team, Denise, Sue, Tiffany, Theo, Shun, Lulu, Angie, and all of my nieces and nephews, thank you for standing by me no matter what! I'm blessed to have you all in my life.

To Allyson Byrd and Jennifer Kem – thank you for pushing me and seeing something in me during a period in my life where I was so frazzled that I couldn't even see straight. You ladies helped me to reignite the warrior within me. I wish a lifetime of blessings to you both!

To the countless women that I've already served, coached, and mentored and the millions of ladies that I have yet to meet, may this book invoke you to play a bigger game and quit the things that no longer serve you. Here's to you prospering from your inner talents and tapping into your riches within!

To My Dear Sister Bernice, thank you for being my special personal angel. I know that you are smiling down on me from heaven.

Love, Light, and Success,
Brandy Butler

Introduction

This book isn't about QUITTING it's about WINNING.

Let's be clear – Don't go out and quit your job prematurely and come back yelling "Brandy told me to JUST QUIT!"

I want you to go through your process intelligently. I also want you to know that I have no paycheck for you. I have plenty of hugs, wisdom and enlightenment to share with you, but no check. It's important that you understand that there are already riches inside of you. It's time to live in your overflow.

Now that I have your attention, I want you to understand that your ultimate goal should not just be about quitting your job but about you winning and mastering the game of SELF. This book is going to help you to begin doing just that.

You see, launching the business is easy. However in order to succeed in your life and business there is a process that you must go through, and while this book will give you extremely valuable tips and strategies, it cannot outline what your process will be, for each woman's journey is different and custom-made by the creator.

"When you find your path, you must not be afraid. You need to have sufficient courage to make mistakes. Disappointment, defeat, and despair are the tools God uses to show us the way."

— Paulo Coelho, Brida

This book will arm you with the strategies and mindset that will help you transition from employee to entrepreneur. Even if you decide that you don't want to own a business, this book will help you to identify your purpose so that you can begin to experience bliss and learn how to incorporate more activities into your life that bring you joy.

I've worked with and mentored hundreds of people across the globe and I've found that many of us already know what it is that we truly want to do. We are just too afraid to step into it. Years of faulty programming and false humility has trained us to lead a life of smallness. As young girls we are taught to be nice and not be bossy. In return we grow into adult women who play small. We sit on the sidelines cheering for the successes of everyone else.

In order to reach your full purpose and step into who you were called to be, here are some things that you must be willing to quit:

Lack of Confidence

FEAR

People Pleasing

Procrastinating

Playing Small

Holding on to Being BROKE

Staying trapped in Brokenness

Staying busy with the wrong activity

Willingly surrounding yourself with negative people

Ignoring your intuition

Envy

Hatred

Focusing on lack

Being more of a consumer than a producer

Low balling your self-worth

Searching for outside validation

I can tell you this with full confidence because these are all obstacles that I've had to overcome in my own life and business. Some of these points I still have to battle on a regular basis.

"People often say that motivation doesn't last. Well, neither does bathing, that's why we recommend it daily."

— Zig Ziglar

Like many women in my generation, I was taught to go to college and get the good job so that I could have the fancy house and car. AND THAT'S EXACTLY WHAT I DID. I became an overachiever constantly working toward moving up the corporate ladder, buying my first home when I was 25, riding around in fancy cars and walking around with expensive designer bags, just to prove that I had made it. Don't get me wrong, there is nothing wrong with liking fine things. However, at the time I was completely overcompensating for my lack of fulfillment and spending based on ego

The truth was that my soul was dying on the inside. I eventually felt trapped at my job. I ended up reaching such a high level on my pay scale that the only way for me to reach the next level would be to lead a team. Honestly I did not want to do that. I was totally uninterested in my IT career and wanted to transition to something more creative and people-based like marketing. The problem was that the marketing jobs that I qualified for were several pay grades below mine. I often ran into situations where the hiring managers loved me, but I already made too much.

So I put on my superwoman cape and participated in every single charity and special cause committee that I could at work. I loaded myself with advanced work training courses because somehow, some way, I was determined that I would enjoy the work that I performed.

When I began to focus on becoming an entrepreneur and creating my own fulfilling work, the flame lit inside of me. The pursuit of entrepreneurship has been a catalyst for strengthening my faith. I was raised in church, and have always been spiritual, but I have never known God like this.

There were times where the turmoil of working a job I hated versus being able to run my "dream" business full-time has caused me immense frustration. What I've come to learn is that this is a faulty lens and perspective for female parallel-preneurs (parallel-preneur: working a full time job while running a business) to have.

I know what it's like to sit in your cubicle feeling as if you are going to snap at any given moment. I know what it's like to have red puffy eyes because you have been crying for something more out of life.

I know what it's like for you to hear that dreaded alarm clock and hitting snooze because you aren't ready to face another lousy work day.

I know what it's like to just want to QUIT.

Hold tight and have faith. You will get there. The law of polarity states that there cannot be a problem without an existing solution. You are just one shift away from your solution.

Here's what I know: everything that you need is already inside of you. There are an abundance of resources available to us once we begin to stand in our "Yes." This book will help you to make the powerful transitions in life that you deserve!

"And, when you want something, all the universe conspires in helping you to achieve it."

— Paulo Coelho, The Alchemist

PART ONE: PREPARING YOUR MIND TO QUIT

1

How My Very First Business Got Shut Down

"You Were Not Born to Become a Dope Dealer's B★tch"
— Mildred Pendleton, My Mama
"Brandy, what is this?"

"What? What are you talking about?" I asked, with my brain still hazy and my eyes bloodshot red. I woke up to find my mother standing above my bed. "What? What are you talking about?" I said, because I was upset, I was sleeping well and here she comes and has the audacity to wake me up out of my good sleep. Then all of a sudden she started shaking me violently.

"Dammit--I said--what is this?" She asked, as she dangled the bags of marijuana over my head.

"What? What? What are you talking about? Ohh." *Oh shit*, I thought to myself as I became conscious. She found my weed. You see, I had the wonderful idea of becoming a marijuana seller--a dope dealer if you will--and I was damn good at it too. Back when I was in high school, I actually used to be what you call a "weed head." It's sad, but true. The whole clique of kids that I hung with smoked weed. As a matter of fact, we called ourselves the BSC, which was short for the Bud Smoking Clique.

Well, even as a teenager, my entrepreneurial mind started to run free and I thought to myself, "Hey, instead of me just spending my money on this all the time, I could make a profit." At the time I was dating a well-known drug dealer. He was a pretty boy, and I got a massive cut on my pricing. I actually was selling a quarter pound of weed, which isn't huge by any means but it was huge for me at the time, and I was doing really well with my sales. Since I already was into that crowd, I understood that niche. I had a great attitude and a lot of people loved to hand out with me. I would cut deals with people, even matching them a sack and smoking with them. How often do you get the opportunity for that type of job, where you get to sell products to people and be entertained by utilizing them, basically for free?

On this particular day, I had done very well with my sales. As a matter of fact, I had a celebratory smoke with my niece--because the day had gone so well. So, I had just finished celebrating a big win, I had a huge day of sales and my niece and I--we were 16 and 17 at the time--were riding around town in my new car excited about the day's events. The product that we had was damn good. I dropped her off at home and went home and feel asleep because that's how potent the marijuana was; but I didn't fall asleep before counting my money. I had been counting my money and thinking about how well the day was going and I thought to myself how rich I was going to be from selling this FIRE product. But there was one problem. The weed made me lazy, and in my haze, I forgot to hide my stash. I fell asleep in the basement of my home which was where my room was located at the time, and then-- *oh shit*! My mother found me, and was yelling violently at me, and the thoughts were flashing through my head, "How could I be so stupid to fall asleep with all of these weed sacks on my chest?" Now granted, I only had an ounce of sacks on my chest, which at that time was about 10 sacks, so I was lucky that she didn't know what a full stash was.

"Brandy, how could you do this to us? Your father and I did not raise you like this. God told me to come down here and check on you, and you know I never come down here." Which was true. I freaked out because I believed that God had sent her. My mother NEVER did come down to the basement to check on me which is why I thought I could get away with what it was that I was doing.

"Your father and I did not raise you to be some dope dealer's bitch."

Her words cut like a knife. Tears started flooding down my face, because I felt like I had disappointed my mother, and I was living below my standards. All I could think to myself was, "I'm so glad that she didn't find the entire stash. She would've freaked if she saw the entire quarter pound of weed."

Now this didn't end well because I had a Bible-thumping mother who did not play, so we ended up fighting. Well, she ended up fighting me is more like it. She went to blows with me; slapped me, punched me, beat the dope dealer's bitch up out of me, and broke my prized necklace at the time. This was the 1990s and in St. Louis we used to wear these big fancy necklaces called add-a-bead chains. They were collectible. You would collect all of these different gold, Chinese-style beads and the size of your add-a-bead chain was like your rite-of-passage. The bigger the add-a-bead chain, and the more unique your beads, the more successful you were or the more street cred you had, and I was just to the point where my add-a-bead chain was getting up there. It was getting attention, and just like that it was ruined because I had chosen to be some dope dealer's bitch. And not because I was raised like that, but that's what I was FAMILIAR with.

I was familiar with that process of selling drugs through the neighborhood that I lived in. Sure I lived in the suburbs, but I lived in a suburb of University City which was well known for being a well-dressed and very materialistic neighborhood. I didn't learn the drug lifestyle from my parents. I lived in a suburban household, my father was a successful businessman, but I wanted to mirror myself after what I saw in my neighborhood, at my school and in pop culture.

Pause: How many times in your life have you lowered your standards just to fit in?

I used to do this all the time. In high school, I would always test high and my best friend and I would test into the honors classes, only to take ourselves out of those classes because that's where the "nerds" were. We would take ourselves out of the honors classes and then put ourselves in the average classrooms so we could hang out with the cool kids.

How many times have you lowered your standards because it was what was FAMILIAR? How many times have you decreased your vision just so that you could fit in with what everyone else is doing? Listen, a lot of times we have a special calling on our lives but for whatever reason we feel like we have to fit in with the norm. As female entrepreneurs, many of us hold ourselves back by trying to fit in. We feel like our business has to fit in with what everyone else is doing when that isn't what God has set up for us. We are trying to fight against what God has promised us.

I thank God that my mother found me when I was on that road to becoming a drug dealer, because that's not the path that God had laid out for me. I also am thankful that my mother found out that I was a weed head at the time, because with her bringing God into the mix, I was never able to smoke weed to that extent again. That ended my weed head days. I've never been able to indulge in marijuana to the extent that I did when my mother told me that God tapped on her, because I know that was divine intervention.

Think about the times that divine intervention has saved your life. Think about the calling that God has on your life. Act accordingly by getting into agreement with what has been promised to you. We will talk about that more throughout this book.

2

How I "Just Quit"

"I bargained with Life for a penny, And Life would pay no more, however I begged at evening when I counted my scanty store. For Life is a just employer, He gives you what you ask, but once you have set the wages, why, you must bear the task. "I worked for a menial's hire, only to learn, dismayed, that any wage I had asked of Life, Life would have willingly paid."

— *My Wage*, Jessie B. Rittenhouse

Enjoy the journey. You must enjoy the journey because you don't know the final destination. You never know how it's going to end. We can assume and we can have a vision of how we want things to go, but a lot of times, we end up having to take the winds in the road. That's why it's important to have a goal, but not to be too attached to what it looks like at the end because a lot of times it's going to look a lot different than how you envisioned it would once you get there.

When I think back to how I got started with my whole entrepreneurial journey, there was no way for me to know that things were going to turn out the way that they have thus far. My path toward entrepreneurship started as a hobby. I had just left a job I held for over 11 years at one of the largest financial firms in St. Louis I had gotten to a place where I was tired of my current position.

A Career Move

I was working in IT and I desperately wanted to move over to the marketing side, however in doing that, I was going to have to take a significant pay cut. At many corporate agencies, IT professionals get paid much more than people in other career fields, something that was also true of this employer.

But I was willing to take the pay cut because I knew that, deep in my heart, marketing is what I wanted to do. As a matter of fact, when I was in college, I actually minored in marketing. My major was Computer Information Systems with Marketing minor. And I was one class, three credits away, from getting my minor in marketing when my father got tired of paying my college tuition and said, "Girl, you better bring your ass home. Nobody cares about minors in this day and age anyway."

I've always loved marketing but I let that minor go and I went into IT mainly because of the income. I knew that I wanted to make a certain level of income and IT was the best way for me to do that. I was able to do that for about 11 years. I kept moving up in the company. I never had a problem with getting raises and promotions. I just got to a place where I was tired. I was bored; I couldn't stay awake in meetings.

At one point, it got so hard for me to stay up during the meetings at work that I started to take my son's ADD pills. At the time, the doctor was trying to put my son on ADD medicine and I thought to myself, "Well, let me test this out before I give it to him," because I was very scared to give him any type of drugs. With the statistics around young males and drug use, I didn't want to give my son anything that I wouldn't be willing to take.

I tested out his ADD medicine and it turns out that I liked it and needed it. At least I felt like I needed it in order to stay up. You see, I didn't want to nod off in meetings, but that's how drained and bored I had gotten with that particular position.

To ward off the boredom, I immersed myself in all types of extracurricular activities at work. Any extra committee, any type of community effort, any activity board, I was on it because I needed something that would fulfill me other than my current role, which I was desperate to get out of.

I kept going up for job after job with no success. Either the pay wasn't enough or I would go through several interviews with boards of five to 10 people, make it all the way to the end and then the other candidate would beat me out.

Eventually I just got tired of being there and a new job came my way. It paid less, but I was willing to take the pay cut just to find some type of fulfillment. My soul was screaming out that I needed something different. So I took the pay cut and moved to a new employer.

Now, I took this pay cut thinking that it would be the thing to do as long as I could enjoy the work and as long as new opportunities came my way. But, boy was I wrong. When I got to this new employer, there weren't many opportunities. And the bonuses that they lured me with, saying that they provided more bonuses than more than my former employer, turned out to be lackluster. It turned out that they did have as many bonuses as my old employer, but they were substantially lower.

I didn't enjoy my new job. I was mad at myself for taking a pay cut. I didn't feel like I had necessarily made a mistake because of how emotionally bankrupt I had been at my old employer. But I knew that I did not like my new employer. I knew that I didn't even want to feel like I was part of the culture there.

A Hobby Becomes a Career

The new job came with one benefit. Since my job load was lighter, I now had time for hobbies. So I went ahead and started making jewelry; handmade jewelry, because I've always been a creative being. Around this time, reality TV really started popping off and "Basketball Wives" had come onto the scene. On the very first season of "Basketball Wives," the ladies had all of this custom jewelry. The cast wore these big hoop earrings with special beads and bracelets that were made by their own designers and I thought to myself, "I could do that. You know, I'm creative, I've always liked making stuff."

I picked up my creativity from my mom. I like to call her Bob Vila because she has always been crafty. So I thought, "I could do this." I started taking jewelry classes and it turns out that I did so well with making jewelry to that people started saying, "You should sell this." I would take pictures of what I had made and people would ask if they could buy it. Even though I didn't start off making jewelry for anyone to buy, I started selling my jewelry online and as soon as I started posting pictures, there was a high demand for it. People just started buying it.

The demand for it made me think that it could really turn into something. And with that, I created a Facebook business page and a beautiful website using Bizzy Mama Hosting, which makes it super easy to create your online store and make it look professional. I was able to surprise people out of the gate because of the professional look of my website and my branding.

The jewelry business picked up fast and before I knew it, I started to have international clients. I also started selling t-shirts that displayed cute natural hair sayings because that's when the natural-hair-saying movement first started booming.

I teamed up with natural hair bloggers and beauty bloggers and more. I would give them my products, they would do reviews, and they would bring me even more visibility and customers. Before I knew it, I had local boutiques in St. Louis asking if they could sell my products. I was selling my products out of jewelry stores and wholesaling my products at beauty salons in town. It was amazing. I had people contacting me from different states asking me to sponsor trade shows. That business grew super-fast.

However, I always knew that there was something more for me. I fell in love with entrepreneurship and with online marketing. From that jewelry business, I was able to understand the power of online marketing. Just from me posting a picture and transitioning to the point where I had a website serving international customers, I learned the power of marketing and online media. From there, I knew that I needed to learn every single thing that I could about online marketing.

Just my business was blowing up, a surprise re-routed my path. I had a record sales month. There was a very popular blogger sharing my page and advertising for me and my sales had just skyrocketed past any milestone that I had ever hit. Then all of a sudden, I started getting exhausted. It wasn't like me, because I am an Energizer Bunny. I mean, I am a workhorse. I love to work. I like to keep it moving, I don't like to just be still. So I knew that there was something wrong, because instead of being ecstatic about filling orders, I was jazzed up about taking naps and calling it a night by 8pm.

It turns out I was pregnant!

Getting pregnant with our third child left me both happy and sad. I was happy to be expecting a child, but I was sad because I thought that my business was going to be my road out of corporate America. I could not wait to leave the corporate world, and once the sales started coming in, my husband started to believe that my dream could become a reality. But once we saw the positive pregnancy test, he was like, "Yes!" And I was like, "Damn," because I knew that I was not in the position to be able to leave my job with us being pregnant.

But one thing that happened with that pregnancy was that I got clear about what I was doing. I loved the jewelry and it was selling well. My t-shirts were selling like hotcakes. I had even gotten to the point where I had wood-branded earrings with my customized logo. But I had to get real with myself. I was tired! I was missing out on life-- birthday parties and spending time with my friends--because I had to physically make these custom jewelry orders. My exhaustion was real.

Using what I had learned earning my MBA, I realized that the jewelry business wasn't scalable. This realization let me know that I needed to let it go and do something else. I also did not want to have a house full of beads and metals and stones with a young baby around who could potentially put my inventory into her mouth!

I had been working with a business coach and she told me, "Brandy, there's so much more here for you. You just have to step into it." So I let that business go because there was something more for me. I got real with myself and I understood that I was meant to inspire people. I wanted to get back to that goal of inspiring young people, young women and teens. I wanted to let them know that who they are is enough and that there is so much potential for success out here as long as they just have the confidence and the gusto to reach for it. Once I let the business go, I was able to get clear with this goal.

Letting Go Helped Me Gain Clarity

My first thought was to start a not-for-profit business for teens. At the time, I didn't realize that you could be inspirational and motivational while making a profit. I thought that the only way to have a motivational business and help others was to do it through a non-profit. Boy, was I wrong!

One of the best things that I did was before I got too deep into the not-for-profit, I hired a not-for-profit consultant. By the time she finished with me and she broke things down, I remember being extremely stressed out and having a headache. Eventually I realized that having a non-profit just was not for me. It's a very noble thing to do and I give anyone props that does it, but it was not a match for my personality type and my energy.

I let the not-for-profit go, but through starting and letting go of both businesses, I gained some valuable lessons. I had the chance to witness how entrepreneurs live because I was working with different consultants from the not-for-profit arena and it gave me a whole new sense of purpose and understanding of how there are so many different revenue streams available in this world, as long as you have the vision and the wherewithal to go out and research and learn more. I learned to look beyond my personal lens.

I Began to Play a Bigger Game

I loved online marketing so much and because I had worked with a business coach who told me, "Hey, you should blog in order to grow your business," I started focusing on online marketing again and blogging. Now I knew that I definitely wanted my online business to be the thing to get me out of corporate America. By the time I had my daughter, I was clear on this. And I didn't want to just flounder around with it.

I hired another coach, Danyelle Little, also known as Cubicle Chick, and it was one of the best things I had ever done. You see, while I sold jewelry, I actually had bartered with Cubicle Chick by sending her some jewelry in exchange for a blogging class that she was teaching.

That's what happens when you take a step of faith. You end up connecting with people and having relationships with people who you never knew existed before and you never know how those relationships are going to turn out. Back when I took her class, I had no idea that the internet marketing and blogging things were so deep. But from her class, Cubicle Chick really showed me the possibilities of working with sponsors and of making money blogging. The possibilities were endless and my head was buzzing.

Fast forward to a year later, after I had my daughter, I knew that Cubicle Chick was the woman that I wanted to work with to help me get set up and established as a professional blogger. So I hired her as my coach. That was one of the best things that I did. The Cubicle Chick plugged me into her network. That's what happens when you step out on faith and you reach out to someone for help. If they're a solid individual and your energies vibe, you have the potential of being plugged into their network and circle of influence.

Fortunately, I won tickets from the Cubicle Chick's blog to attend my very first blogging conference, the Niche Parent (which is now the Niche Network). Once there, I was immersed into an atmosphere full of internet marketers and lifestyle bloggers. This was completely new for me, but for the people I was around, this was their everyday life.

I felt like I had just fallen into a secret society full of entrepreneurs making a legitimate living from online business. I knew that I was in the right place. When you step out on faith, and keep walking in it, God will put you in the places where he wants you to thrive. He will place you among the people who will show you how to take your vision and your life to the next level.

I learned as much as I could about blogging and internet marketing. I knew that this was going to be the business for me. It was like a light; a fire was burning inside of me because now I knew how to combine the best pieces of me. I was able to leverage all of my years in IT and merge it with the creativity that had always lived inside of me. I loved online business. I loved blogging. I just still didn't understand yet how exactly I was going to make a sustainable business.

Help was on the way.

One thing that I've always been good at is getting help and learning. I have an insatiable desire to learn, and when you are a learner, you're an earner. This is the best way to increase your income. It's to have a willingness to go out and learn more about whatever it is that you want to do.

I started taking online marketing courses. I started reading every book I could. I read blog posts. I watched webinars. I just absorbed as much information as I could. Eventually, I knew that this path would take me toward what I wanted to do full-time.

During this time, I learned about the law of attraction and *The Secret* and vision boards and visualization. When I learned about *The Secret*, I fell in love with Lisa Nichols, one of the world's leading Transformational Breakthrough Specialists. I absolutely fell in love with her. I loved the whole entire cast from the movie, but by Lisa Nichols being the only black woman in the movie, she resonated with me. She pierced my heart. I knew that I wanted to learn more about her and to get a chance to experience her in person.

I put Lisa Nichols' picture on my vision board and hosted a vision board party at the beginning of 2014. The following week, I wrote out my business plan and on it I wrote that I would become a professional speaker and that I would be professionally trained by Lisa Nichols.

I didn't necessarily know what that meant at the time. I had been unable to attend all of the other conferences that she had hosted, for one reason or another. Either I had been pregnant or the finances didn't work out.

As soon as I became clear that I wanted to be trained by Lisa Nichols, I received an unexpected extra check in the mail. When it came unexpectedly, I asked myself and the Lord how I was supposed to use this check. By that time we were already a family of five, so Lord knows we always had bills. But I knew that I needed to do something different with it. I knew that I needed to sow this seed in a way that I had never sowed it before.

When you want something different, you have to do things differently. If you want to experience something different, you have to do something that you've never done before. Up until that point, I had never been to a Lisa Nichols conference. Sure, I had been to other self-development conferences. I had been to all types of blogging and industry conferences, but I had never been to a Lisa Nichols conference. Up to that point, I had never met someone who I held at such a high esteem.

I gave myself the permission to buy my ticket to the Lisa Nichols event. For three months, I waited excitedly to go see Lisa Nichols. Luckily I had an extra ticket, so I was also able to bring one of my fellow girlfriend entrepreneurs along.

By this time, I had moved on to a contract position at another company because I had several breakdowns at the job that I had accepted after my long-time employer. I HATED that job. When I got the unexpected opportunity to become a contractor at another company making excellent money, I took it! I knew that I was not going to be working for anyone else for very long anyway. "By the time this contract ends, it's time for me to be out on my own," I told myself.

That is how I felt on the inside, but honestly, I was not structurally prepared to be without a job. However, a small voice just told me to keep going to work. So I kept going to the new job even though I hated it, too. I was tired of my career as a whole. It didn't matter which company I moved to; I had simply outgrown the type of work I had been doing for the previous 15 years. In the meantime, I kept blogging. I had a lot of friends at this job, but I stopped socializing and taking lunch with people. I viewed my lunch hour as a crucial component to my cubicle exodus and used every single minute of it to work on my business. I kept growing my business while I worked. Finally the day of the Lisa Nichols event had arrived.

I felt like it was my destiny to get to the Lisa Nichols event in San Diego, California. I didn't know what was going to happen there, but I knew that God had something special for me once I got there.

The day before the Lisa Nichols event, my car broke down. I ended up getting a flat tire and I couldn't make it to work. Actually, a series of strange occurrences happened that day. Life is funny like that. Many times when we are close to experiencing a breakthrough, we will encounter distractions in an effort to discourage us from pursuing our destiny. When this happens to you, I want you to PUSH through, don't get distracted by a current circumstance, and don't distort your truth.

Once I finally made it to the airport, I was waiting to board the airplane in 10 minutes when I got the call from my contract agency that my job was over. I was laid off. I was told that I had done nothing wrong; they just did not need my position anymore.

I wasn't sad. I couldn't even bring myself to cry. Stunned would be an accurate description. I didn't know what to do because I had never lost a job before. I had never been fired or laid off. But I knew that God's hand was in the mix for me to have Lisa Nichols on my vision board and then for me to lose my job on the way to this event that I felt like was so momentous in my life. I knew that there was a hidden blessing in it.

The Lisa Nichols event was phenomenal. It was life-changing. I received everything that I needed to hear in that moment at the event. Before that event, I had attended conferences that were all about technology and strategy. But a lot of what Lisa Nichols taught me hit my soul, especially as an entrepreneur. Going to her conference helped me to see the full picture of entrepreneurship. My mindset as an entrepreneur was forever shifted.

If you're someone who knows that you want more, but feels like there is a piece that's missing or that something hasn't been clicking, I encourage you to travel to different cities and experience conferences. You will be immersed in a whole new thought process, you will meet new people and you will gain valuable connections. Some of the people that I met at that conference became business partners of mine and I ended up collaborating with them. I also left Lisa Nichols' conference with two world-class coaches - one for marketing and the other for profit and sales. Both of these dynamic women helped me to create true power in my business.

Both of my coaches taught me how to position myself as an expert and an authority. That mere shift in mindset helped me to move from a place where my prior blogging business had been anchored in sponsorships and waiting on someone to choose me for a campaign to being an entrepreneur, pursuing clients, telling people about my offer, having an elevator speech and knowing how to position and package myself. By investing in myself, I switched my mindset and I was able to work with coaches who were able to stand in the gap with me and show me how to better structure my business.

"Most women are programmed to spend money on clothes, hair, and shoes. Many women don't realize that if they were to take that same money they waste on material things, objects that are fleeting, and use it on a business coach, personal development program, or conference instead, how much their lives would be enriched and how much closer they would be towards living their dreams."

— Brandy Butler

So that's how I got started as a full-time entrepreneur. I ended up laid off and I was put in a position of sink or swim. That's what it takes for some people. A lot of people want to leave their jobs, they want to work in the field of their passions, but it's scary. It's terrifying to think of leaving your job when you have been in a place that's been so stable for so long; where you're provided for and know on a regular basis that you've got a check. Many of us have kids, we have spouses, we have mates, we have homes, and we have responsibilities. It is very scary to just take the leap, but sometimes the leap is simply what it takes.

I never would have taken the leap on my own. I'll tell you, it's been a journey and I'm loving every minute of it. Even the times where it's gotten dark. I've always risen up bigger and better than before. Some of my greatest lessons have been in the dark spaces.

Maybe you're going through a period in your life where it's dark. What I want you to know is that you will rise up. It's up to you to learn what you were supposed to learn while you were in a valley and then become better.

If you want to learn more about your possibilities as an entrepreneur or want to experience a shift in your business, I invite you to apply for a complimentary breakthrough session with me: _http://brandybutleronline.com/breakthrough_

Take One Step...

If you're a woman who wants to take her life to the next level and create a business, just take one step. Take one imperfect action and get started. Don't worry about people saying that you're all over the place. Don't worry about shifting. You have to do all of that. You have to just start and then shift.

It doesn't matter how many books you read, you will not know how to do certain things until you are actually doing them. This is all part of the journey and everyone's journey is different, unique and special. So just take one step. Be open to the process. Stay aware and continue learning. That is how my journey started.

You're looking at someone who started out as an IT professional, became a jewelry designer and has been able to transform herself into an entrepreneur, motivational speaker and now author. So what's your next? Get clear on it, because you can fast track. You don't have to waste time doing the practice brands like I did. I like to think of my jewelry business as being a practice brand. Maybe you don't even have to go through a practice brand. Here's the thing; you can get very clear now and be real with yourself about what it is that you want to do.

Don't worry about how grand it seems. Just worry about whether or not it is the thing that you really want to do. Do whatever it is that is your heart's desire. You've done whatever everyone else has wanted you to do all this time. Now is the time for you to stand in your "Yes," get clear and do what it is that you really want to do. In the next chapter, I'll discuss more about the importance of being clear with yourself on what you desire.

For More Inspiration and Business Building Information, Check Out My Site: *http://brandybutleronline.com*

3

The Power of Clarity

"Thoughts become things. If you see it in your mind, you will hold it in your hand."

— Bob Proctor

Holding onto my job made me crazy. I tried and tried to hold onto my job but at some point, my disdain for my job would still bubble up, and it finally got to the point to where I couldn't take it anymore. I walked off my job a couple of times and my doctor actually told me to leave my job, but I wasn't at the financial place where I could. My doctor told me that I needed to figure things out and she scheduled time with a therapist for me.

I started to get job stress therapy in order to help me to cope with the strain of being on my job, managing my family and being nine months pregnant. Let me tell you, therapy is one of the best things that happened in my life, because not only did I have the stress of my job, I had additional family members staying with me, which added the dynamic of trying to manage two families, stress from my parents and other family issues. What therapy helped me to realize was that I wasn't crazy. I was actually very sane. There were just temporary circumstances that were placed on me that were too much for me to handle. The load was too heavy and I needed tools and strategies to be able to handle that type of stress.

Working with my therapist helped me to gain a clear vision of myself and not just the views that were put on me by my co-workers, by my manager who thought I was freaking out and by my husband, who didn't understand how I felt at the time. Working with a therapist helped me to get outside of myself and see myself very clearly.

If you're at a point where your job stress and your personal life are too much for you to handle, I urge you to get the help that you need. See a therapist and have him or her help you. Allow them to give you coping strategies and emotional support that you can't gain within yourself, that you can't gain from the church and that you can't gain from your family or friends or support system. Don't be afraid to ask for help when you need it. There's help out there. You don't have to deal with the stress that you're dealing with by yourself.

Name Your Treasure

Clarity is so very, very important in your business because you need to be extremely clear about what it is that you want to achieve and how you are going to go about doing so. As a matter of fact, you don't even have to know the how, but you do need to know the what. If you've ever researched characteristics of successful people and looked at materials written by different thought leaders such as Brian Tracy, Bob Proctor or Napoleon Hill of *Think and Grow Rich*, the way that you become successful is by having a definite purpose. You need to be clear about what it is you want to do. What is your next step when you leave this job or this career that you've had enough of?

We are all creators. Our creator put us here on Earth so that we could create as well. You have infinite power inside of you and many of us just have not known how to tap into that power. We've been so institutionalized from the time we were children. First, our parents told us what we could and what we couldn't do. Then we went to school had to follow the rules and regulations. We went on to work at different jobs and had to follow the rules and the regulations that were structured by our bosses, our corporations or our institutions. As an entrepreneur, you get a chance to create your own rules.

I want you to look at the world through a different lens. I want you to get clear about what it is that you want to create. Now, if you're brand new to this journey, this is going to seem like a very large task for you and it is. But the way that you can chunk this down is by taking a self-assessment and thinking about what it is that you've always loved to do.

I call this "Name Your Treasure." What is the treasure that's buried inside of you? It's time for you to unlock that treasure and share it with the world. Are you someone who's extremely crafty? Are you creative? Do you have a knack for making things look beautiful? Are you someone who wants to be a stylist or an interior decorator or an event planner? What are the things that you have always naturally been inclined to do? Is that your next venture? The next step for you is to take that vision and make something out of it.

Often the things we like to do are right in front of us. Your talents are paving the way for what's next for you, especially as a woman looking to enter the marketplace. What are your unique talents? What have you naturally been gifted with? When you build a business, you want to create it based on your talents. You don't want to build a business on a skill that takes you too much time for you to learn.

Now, you're always going to be learning and you're always going to be adding to your skill repository, but you don't want to base your business in an area where you're weak. You want to build upon your strengths because if you can really build upon and leverage your strengths, you're going to be able to gain momentum. You're going to go faster and it's going to create that platform and create that energy that you need in order to gain the confidence and get the success that you are trying to attain.

Step One: Think Back to Your Childhood

One of the ways that you can assess your talents is to think back to your childhood. What is it that you liked to do as a child? Who did you pretend to be? What did you want to be when you grew up?

When I was a young girl, I wanted to an artist, because I used to love to draw. But I always envisioned myself as a business woman. I'm a late 70's baby, so I'm an 80's kid. We didn't have a computer yet, so I would make a computer for myself using an Etch-A-Sketch screen and make the keyboard out of Legos to envision myself in the office.

That's who I am today. I'm a business woman. I love business. I always have, as a child and as an adult. When I really had to take time to assess who I was, back when I was in a corporate job and I was searching for myself, I really had to look at my skills and who it is that I've always wanted to be.

You need to really get clear on who it is that you want to be, because you have to start taking the steps toward becoming that person now. You can't hold who you want to be in a dream space. A dream space becomes a gap that is hard to close when you leave too many of your goals there.

You have to make your dreams a reality by moving out of a place of becoming and transitioning into a state of being. Who will you be? A life coach? A success coach? A boutique owner? An author? Whoever it is that you've always wanted to be, now is the time for you to start referring to yourself as that person, get some business cards created that reflect that title and start introducing the world to you. That way when you go out and you network with people and you introduce your business, you've established yourself in a very professional way and a very solid way. Don't hold it in a dream space, actualize it and start referring to yourself as the person you want to be. That's what creates momentum.

Step Two: Get Personal Feedback

Another thing that you can do in order to get clear and to make sure that you're on track is to get feedback from some trusted resources. I want you to be careful when you go and get this feedback. Make sure that you are not asking people who are inherently negative. This is a very fragile time in your business. You're building your business and trying to come into who it is that you want to become, so you need some people who are going to speak life into you. There is nothing wrong with constructive criticism and with objective feedback, but this is not the time for that. You can get that later, once your business has been established. At that time, you can get some constructive feedback from your clients and the people that you serve.

Right now, in the very beginning, you are just trying to figure out your structure and give birth to your vision. If you know that you have an inherently negative friend, relative or colleague, do not include them in this exercise. Do not include them in your plans for the future because you don't want to shut down your future before you even have a chance to breathe life into it. Your vision is fragile. It's like a newborn baby and you need people who will be able to treat it gently and breathe life into it.

Again, go and contact some trusted resources, ask them a series of about 5-10 questions. Here are some examples:

1. What do you see me doing?
2. What do I seem like I am happiest doing?
3. What's something that you can always count on me for?
4. How would you describe me?
5. What is an area in which you think I excel?

Ask at least 10 people. Send them an e-mail, and then follow up with them within a week for their answers. Compile those answers and evaluate them against what you believe is your personal truth. You will be surprised how often the answers of your friends, family and colleagues reflect what you have already determined. Their reflections just offer some helpful reinforcement for your own self-discovery.

Step Three: Take a Personality Test

Another way to find out your talents and strengths is to take a personality test. There are many types of personality tests. I am a big advocate of the StrengthsFinder test. You may have done this type of test before as an employee, but it's a very different experience when you are doing it for yourself as a practice of self-awareness. As an entrepreneur and a person who's trying to get closer to her purpose and really get centered at her core, I definitely suggest that you take it again so that you can evaluate it along with all of the other information that you have compiled.

Now it's time for you to analyze these components:

- What is it that I used to enjoy doing as a child?
- What feedback did I get from my friends and my trusted sources?
- What do I think about myself and my gifts?
- What were the results of my personality test?

Once you have all of this information, you're armed with what you need to start crafting your next step: getting the knowledge to begin building your platform.

Take a Moment to Reflect

- What are the activities that bring you the most joy?
- What is your heart's desire?
- If you could make excellent money doing anything you wanted, what would you choose to do?

_____

_____

_____

_____

_____

_____

_____

_____

_____

_____

_____

_____

_____

_____

_____

_____

_____

_____

_____

_____

_____

4

Stop Living and Branding on the Sideline

"There is only one thing that makes a dream impossible to achieve: the fear of failure."

— Paul Coelho

I want to talk to you about a plague. A disorder that it pains me to see so many people around me suffering from. I can't stand for people suffering from it to be around me. It's called sitting around on the sidelines and just watching.

I thought about this because I have so many people asking me about starting their automation processes and attracting more clients online, but they aren't doing the work. Once we have a chance to sit down and talk, they will tell me, "I've heard all of this before, I already know it."

But they aren't doing it! Does this sound like you? You aren't doing the things that you need to do in order to attract clients in order to communicate with them on a regular basis and in order for them to get familiar with your brand. You aren't taking the steps you need to take in order to gain their trust and convert them into buying customers. You may know all of all these things, but you haven't implemented anything.

I find that behavior quite troubling. I'm a woman of action. My friends call me the activator because I take action and if I'm involved in your life, and you're a part of my space, I'm going to make sure that you take action too.

Let's be Clear-Education without implementation is simply entertainment.

If you're investing in coaching programs, Google searching your business idea and listening to podcasts, yet you are not implementing a damn thing, you're simply entertaining yourself. When you hold an idea in a dream state for too long and not take steps to see it as a reality, that idea can't manifest. Now, some people reading this book may be fine with that. Maybe you just need to be entertained, and I'd much rather you be entertained by self-development materials, business building skills and compelling content about creating a better lifestyle for yourself than a reality show. Let's face it, there's so much smut and crap on TV that if you're seeking positive entertainment, then kudos to you. However, if you are seeking this information and this knowledge because you really want to create a better life for yourself then it's time for you to start implementing.

You need to really get serious about implementation, especially if you have been investing your dollars into education. Stop sitting on the sidelines. Go ahead; create that free opt-in bribe or that eBook. Write those email auto-responder series, send out some emails to your newsletter, and grow your newsletter list. Do all of the things that you repeatedly hear that you should be doing to grow your online business, dammit. It's time for you to do it, now!

Don't tell me everything you know, because when you aren't doing anything with it, knowing doesn't make a damn difference. My charge for you is to stop being addicted to acquiring knowledge and start being addicted to applying knowledge.

Apply some of that knowledge and see the difference that it makes in your life. See what difference it will make to your profit center. Start implementing more and stop being on the sidelines.

Now, some of you reading may not have attained enough knowledge. That's okay. There may still be some missing pieces. There is a time and a place for gaining new knowledge and taking action. You may not yet be at a place where you can implement, because you haven't learned. If this is you, I highly suggest that you get the information you need. Invest in yourself. Get some coaching and mentorship. Get involved in an accountability group and find somebody who can be your accountability partner. Place yourself in environments where you can gain new knowledge and get the new skill set that you need. Some things important to our businesses we don't just naturally know. We have to pursue the knowledge.

Having accountability is necessary, because you need someone sometimes to be your cheerleader and to make sure you're staying on track with your goals. They can keep you on task with questions like, "Hey, you said that by January 31st you were going to launch your new website, where are you with that?" "You said by February 14th you were going to launch your new product or your new program. How is that coming along?" "How do you plan on launching it? How are your customers going to get their product fulfillment?"

Having an accountability partner, a coach or a master mind, helps you stay committed to the thing that you said that you were going to do. That's why I have created both of those pieces in my business. I coach clients and help them to create that confidence and clarity so they can know what they are doing with their business and how they're going to implement. Some people who can't afford coaching, or have been coached before and feel like they have attained the right knowledge, if left up to themselves, would not implement what they have learned. For those, we have the mastermind program.

You can find out more about my coaching services. I have free discovery sessions for people that need a little bit of clarity and want to talk things through with someone. If you want to learn more about your possibilities as an entrepreneur or want to experience a shift in your business, I invite you to apply for a complimentary breakthrough session with me *http:brandybutleronline.com/breakthrough*

What I want to leave you with from this chapter is that you've got to get off of the sidelines and start implementing. You will see that the people who implement, whether it's right or wrong, those action-takers are the ones who end up reaping their harvest. It doesn't have to be perfect. You just stay in action and you will be perfected throughout your process. It won't be perfect at first, but you have to act throughout your imperfections and from there, your brilliance will shine. That's where you will connect with people. That's where you will begin to serve people. That's where you will reap your harvest.

5

Have the Faith to Focus

"Lack of direction, not lack of time, is the problem. We all have twenty-four hour days."
— Zig Ziglar

You need faith in order to focus. I know a lot of entrepreneurs, especially women entrepreneurs, want to know how the entire puzzle is going to fit together. We want to know the end result. We like to be in control. Most people do not like to be in a state of questioning and not knowing how the race is going to end, but guess what? You never know how it's going to end. That's why you are perfected through the process.

If you don't have the faith to focus, you'll wind up trying a bunch of different ventures all at once and wear yourself out with frustration when nothing is working. It's kind of like throwing spaghetti up against the wall and figuring out what's going to stick.

You need to focus on one thing at a time. I'm not telling you that you can't have multiple businesses and more than one passion. But starting your business, getting your feet wet, getting the lay of the land and getting acclimated to your new environment is going to take so much out of you that you will need to focus on one thing. Imagine how much more powerful you could be if you focused and centered all of your energy toward one goal instead of spreading yourself out over three or four ventures.

Many clients come to me suffering from a lack of focus. For example, one of my clients is phenomenal; a true boss woman at the executive level of her company. She spreads herself so thin and in the process, runs from the thing that she needs to focus on. She is not unique in this. I see this happening with women all of the time.

We want something to happen, but it seems so big, so grand that we just don't know if it's ever going to happen for us. Sometimes the business is moving so slowly, and it's not picking up at the pace that we want. We're not getting interviewed enough. No one is featuring us. There's not enough buzz about us. In order to handle the frustration, we create an additional brand or create an additional business where we're already struggling with the first business. We're not even leveraging the first business to its full potential before starting a new business that demands just as much or more of our attention. The result is that we become overwhelmed.

The reason why you're overwhelmed is because you're not acting from a place of faith. You are trying to increase your probability, lay out as many path courses as possible to see which path will actually work. You are in a state of busyness and hurry because you lack faith in your ultimate desire. You doubt that thing that you say was your calling, the thing that used to wake you up at night, the thing that you said you would do and that you would not stop; you wouldn't quit no matter what. You lack faith in your calling and as a result you are adding more complexity to it. This is where women lose. This is where entrepreneurs lose because you're focused on trying to beat the odds instead of having faith in your calling.

There's no miracle pill that's going to help you. There's no overnight success. It all takes time. If this is you, if you're falling into this trap, you need to slow down. Breathe. I'm serious; close your eyes, pause, and take a long exhilarating breath right now.

Once you have faith and are focused on what you really want, it becomes easier for you to decline some of the distractions dressed up as opportunities. You can and focus on the main goal so that you can gain traction. You can't do that if you don't have faith in your process. It doesn't work if you are fearful that you're going to lose everything and that you're going to fail.

If you don't have the faith right now, work on exercising your faith muscle. Envision what it is that you really want. Speak it out loud, ask for it and focus on it. This is how you'll beat overwhelm. This is how you keep yourself from being spread too thin.

6

Getting Into Agreement with What Has Been Promised to You

"For I know the plans I have for you," declares the Lord, "plans to prosper you and not to harm you, plans to give you hope and a future."
— Jeremiah 29:11 New International Version (NIV)

In order for you to have faith and focus, you have to come into agreement with what God says about you. Once you come into agreement with what He says about you, and with the vision that has been placed in you and with the desires of your heart, you allow yourself to dream big and not stay logical. You won't look at your dream from a place of lack. You won't say things to yourself like: "Oh, let me scale this down because it doesn't seem logical.""Oh, why would I say I could make six figures in my business? It's my first year.""I could never be a millionaire. None of my family are millionaires. Everybody has been on welfare." Or, "I could never be a millionaire. I'm the first college graduate in my family."

None of those things matter. You have to seize the vision that's within you and the desires of your heart. Give yourself the permission to achieve that level of success and come into agreement with knowing that you are worth it and that you can achieve it. God wants us to be prosperous. He wants us to earn well. When we sow goodness into the world, God wants us to live well, because that's how He gets the glory. He doesn't get the glory from you being broke. Don't look at money as evidence of greed, or believe that only evil, unscrupulous people make a lot of money.

You need money in order to perform good works in the world. You were created to be prosperous. You have millions of riches within you. That's why you have so many talents. You were given those talents so that you could prosper from them.

Affirm: I'm ready to unleash the riches buried within me

If those talents were placed in you from your creator, obviously you have provisions within you that it is time for you to use to live out your purpose, own your worth, stop getting stuck in someone else's greatness, own who you are and allow yourself to step up to be even bigger and grander. This is where it gets a little bit scary, because a lot of women have been taught not to be bossy, to stay humble and to be a team player. When you are doing Kingdom work, when you are doing the work of a visionary, you have to be willing to step up big and bold.

I'm not saying that you have to change your personality and that you have to become someone who is big and brash. What I am saying is that you have to be bold with your gifts, especially in the marketplace. You need to vocalize what it is that you bring to the world, how you can serve people, and how they can get in contact with you. This is the only way that the vision is going to grow. This is the only way that you will be able to serve people. The only way that you will get business is by marketing yourself and letting people know who it is that you are and what you do for the world. The only way that you can do that boldly is by being confident in your skills and that which is destined for you.

It's your destiny to live out your vision. Nobody has to give you permission. You don't have to wait on anyone to say, "You're good enough," or, "You're ready." Let me tell you something, Girlfriend-YOU ARE READY. YOU ARE BEYOND READY. Your time is now! Your time is not off in space. It's right now. Own your greatness, right now. If you're someone who has always second guessed herself and always over-thought every single thing that you've done, I want you to release that. You have enough skills. You have enough talent to do whatever it is that you know that you want to do. And, guess what? Even if it's imperfect at first, you will be able to course correct. You will be able to listen, get feedback, and fix whatever it is that you need to change.

First, you need to have the confidence to start taking those little bitty steps. Get into agreement with what was promised for you. If you know that greatness is in your horizon, you know that you were created to live well, to be generous and to have plenty to give to people. If you know that you were meant to travel across the world, spreading your message, start stepping into that now. We live in a world where the creator not only has created nature but where He has allowed human beings to be creators as well. Do you realize that Thomas Edison created things that began as thoughts in his own mind? There was no evidence that any of those creations were going to appear in the world. They came simply from a vision that was in his mind.

Ford did not know that he was going to be the king of automotives. He just had a vision and then he kept going and kept pushing. And guess what? Along the way he teamed up and partnered with people who were able to believe in his vision and invest, and also mastermind with him so that he could learn the skills that he needed to know, or gain different vantage points in order to grow his business. Think about the Wright brothers. They created an airplane. They were crazy enough to believe that man could fly. There was no evidence that it was possible. They thought it up with their brains. Then, once they had the thought, they were able to manifest it. Now, look at the world. We travel all around the world with the drop of a dime, all because the Wright brothers had the vision.

What vision do you have? Think about that. Don't excuse it. Don't belittle it, because what if you are the next Thomas Edison? The next Ford? The next Wright brothers? You're worth it. You're a creator. Embrace the abundance. Embrace the possibility. Be confident in your gifts. Be confident in your vision, and start taking the steps to making it a reality.

7

How to Silence the Haters

"*Weak and overwhelmed individuals respond to others' success by attacking it.*"

— Grant Cordone

Haters, haters, haters ... We all have haters, right? You always hear people talking about, "Shout out to my haters," or giving so much credit to their haters that their haters really don't even deserve.

Can I tell you a secret, Sis? Guess who your biggest hater is? It's not your arch nemesis from high school. It's not your sister. It's not your cousin. It's not your frienemy. It's *you*. You are your own biggest hater. You might be dismissing this as some kind of self-love talk. But, I'm serious.

We are our worst critics. But in order for you to reach the next level that you are trying to reach, you need to be aware when you are being a big hater to yourself, and you need to understand how to silence that hater.

We get so caught up in thinking about what is possible and viewing things from our own limited lens that often we shoot down our vision. We shoot down our future before it has a chance to even gain legs.

Let me give you an example. Let's say that you want to generate 10,000 dollars in your business this month. Let's say that you are planning to do a big launch in your business, and you tell yourself, "I'm going to make 10,000 this month" but instead of powerfully stating, "I am going to create 10,000 dollars in this month," you say things like, "I hope I can make 10,000 dollars," or, "I really would like to make 10,000 dollars, but I've never been able to make 10,000 dollars in as short of a time period as a month."

No. No. No. You have to speak power into whatever goals that you have. Speak power into them. Speak life into your business, and watch your language. If you just take a step back and actually watch and listen to the words that come out of your mouth, you will understand why you are achieving or why you aren't achieving the level of success that you want. A lot of times it is because of the words that you are speaking about yourself.

If you do not step into your own power, you cannot achieve powerful results. Whenever you get to a point where you find yourself using weak language, I want you to course correct that. Stop in your tracks and start speaking power over your goals, your vision and your business. If you want to make 10,000 in a month, tell yourself, "I am going to make 10,000 this month." Speak power into that. If your goal is to make six figures in this 12-month period, tell yourself, "I am going to make six figures within this year."

Write that number somewhere that you can always see it. Some people write it down every day. If you have a figure that you want to reach, write that down every single day. Speak it. Believe it wholeheartedly, because if you don't believe it, you're going to deter it. If you don't speak positively of the goals that you set forth, you will repel them. You have to come into this place of knowing. You have to feel it. You have to visualize it.

Start manifesting the things that you want to see instead of worrying about the things that you don't want to see. This is why I say that a lot of times we're our own worst haters, because sometimes we are so fixated on what we don't want to happen that we can't even see what we want to happen. If you focus on a problem, you're going to bring more of the problem. If you focus on solutions, you'll start experiencing more solutions.

I love listening to Abraham Hicks. She is a huge thought leader on the subject of law of attraction. She talks about raising your vibration and visualizing something for 17 seconds, and then increasing the vibration of what is that you visualize, and then increase and think of another positive thing for the next 17 seconds, and then increase each time. Think of another positive thing. This is how you manifest.

Even if you are having a down period in your business, you're really stressed out at work or things aren't going well in your relationships at home, don't focus on what is going wrong. Focus on what's going right, so that you can get more of the right. This is not to say that you won't ever feel sad or down, or you won't be stressed out, because you will. Life happens.

What I'm saying is, the way that you can bridge that gap is by not staying stuck in what is going on right now, because that's just a perception, a temporary circumstance. It's just what's in front of you. You have to focus on what it is that you want to create, so that thing can come forth. You have to hold fast to the vision that you have in your head. Instead of saying, "I don't want to do this. I don't want to be like that. I don't want to fail," focus on succeeding. Focus on attaining the six or seven figures that you want. Focus on the accolades. Focus on the love and the joy that you get from doing whatever it is that you want to do in your life and your business.

When I was younger, I had a bunch of aunts who used to talk about their weight all the time. Some of them may have been overweight. Not all of them, but some of them were. I grew up thinking, "I don't want to be like her." That was what I grew up looking at and thinking "I don't want to be like that." You can't focus on what you don't want to be like, because you end up being more like that.

How many of you have ever thought about your parents and said, "Oh, I don't want to be like my mom?" Not to say that your mom is not a great person, because I'm sure she is, but maybe she has some different quirks about her, or some things that you just weren't too fond of. How many times have you ever looked at your parents and said, "I don't want to be like my parents," only to grow up and end up just like them? That's because you focused on what you didn't want.

Instead of focusing on what you don't want, focus on what you want. That's why vision boards are so important, because vision boards help us to stay focused on what we want to create. If you don't have one right now, or maybe your vision board is old, go create a new vision board. Place the things on it that you want. Place the things on it that you dream of. It could be possessions, it could be something that symbolizes the type of success or the type of happiness that you want to have, or it could be a vision board full of words. You need to arm yourself with tools like vision boards in order to manifest the type of life that you want, and keep your eyes on what you want, so that you're not always coming from a place of what you don't want to happen.

Create a vision board. Stay focused on what you want to happen. The Bible says, "Without vision, the people will perish." It's not good enough to say what you want. You have to have a vision. You have to be very clear on what it is that you want to happen, so that that thing can be created, and you need to keep an eye on it by having tools like vision boards or journaling so that you can always go back and look at that thing and be reminded.

This is how you arm yourself. That way, when you are having a bad day you can go back and look at what you want. Focus on what you want so that you can create it. Focus on the solution, not on the problem. If you do that, you can experience more of the solution, and that you can stay in the flow of creating it.

Whenever you get into a place of self-doubt or start thinking that you aren't enough and believing that bold accomplishments can only happen for people like Tyra Banks and Oprah, and that level of success can't happen to little old you, I want you to stop being your own hater. I want you to breathe life into yourself.

State how wonderful you are. Use tools like affirmations. Put the word, "I am" in front of whatever it is that you want to be, even if you don't feel strong enough yet; even if you don't feel like you are that person yet. Start declaring it now. In the Bible, two of the most powerful words are, "I am." There's something special and powerful about saying what you are, and saying, "I am." Instead of downing yourself, instead of being a hater to yourself, start declaring what you are.

Another way that you could be a hater to yourself is by over-thinking things and being in a state of over-perfection. Listen. If you wait until everything is perfect, it's never going to happen. As a matter of fact, you are perfected by the process. Start taking imperfect action, so that you can create perfect momentum.

I'm not saying that you should not shoot for excellence. You absolutely should shoot for excellence. I love the Bible proverb that says, "Lord, bless the work of our hands." You want to make sure that you have poured your spirit, and poured excellence, into anything that you put your hands on. However, you cannot stall and wait on this state of being ready, this state of perfection, because you will never reach it. When you are stalling, and you're not putting forth your body of work, you're not serving the people who you were sent here to serve. It's not fair, because you were sent here to be a release. You are meant to be a light bulb for someone else.

Stop giving away your power. Stop worrying about how everyone else is impacting you or how everybody else is hating or how nobody is supporting you. Start thinking about how you can be your own best cheerleader, how you can stop being your own hater, how you can get out of your way so that you can achieve the level of success that you were created to achieve in the world.

8

Show Up as You Want to Be Seen

"Mostly, the world sees you the way you see yourself."
— Lisa Nichols

In this chapter, I'm going to talk to you about showing up as you want to be seen. You've got to show up, and what I mean by showing up is being clear about who it is that you want to be. This is a recurrent thing that I talk about. Being clear about who it is that you want to be, and how you want to be seen.

False humility, a lot of times, has us show up as someone who's a fan, or an admirer. While it's okay for you to be a cheerleader for someone else and admire their work, you want to be cognizant about how you show up in the world. As a woman, it's so critical, especially if you're an African American or a minority woman, that you stand up in your power. What I mean by this is: whenever you go out, make sure that you're representing your brand well. Make sure that you look the part, professional and crisp, because people will treat you based on their perception of you. This is especially important when you attend conferences or networking events.

If you meet someone whose work you are a fan of, let me give you a tip. Do not run up to them and act like a fangirl, and by fangirl, or fanboy, what I mean is shouting, "Oh my God, I love you, I love you, I love you."

Don't do that. Hold some of that back. Even though you may be thrilled and screaming on the inside, hold in some of that excitement and approach them as a professional. Say, "Hello. Hi, I'm Brandy Butler. I coach women. I help them to gain visibility in their business and package their expertise." Never let them see you sweat. Always arrive as a force and stand in your power.

I know a lot of people will tell you it's important to be transparent, and it is to a certain extent; but some people have to gain or earn your transparency. Everyone is not privy to and does not deserve your transparency, so when you meet different influencers or mentors that you absolutely love, it's very important that you keep your composure and that you don't come across as a fangirl, because the way that they first meet you is how they're going to remember you. They're going to categorize you in a box and treat you as such.

There are some people who are an exception to this. They won't mistreat you, they'll always treat you fairly; but you can show up much more powerfully if you compose yourself. Have your 30-second elevator pitch, introducing yourself, telling people who you are, the services that you bring to the world and how you help people. Come across as a professional, so that people can see you as a professional.

Another way to come off as a professional is by having professional branding, and professional branding does not have to cost a lot. As an example, let's say that you do local events and you have an exhibit at a conference. It is not very expensive for you to just do simple things like go out and buy a nice tablecloth, get maybe some little knickknacks, some little accents and pictures, to decorate your exhibit with, and this goes for whatever industry you're in. Decorate your table, print your cards, and get some nice, thick-stock business cards. I prefer

49

MOO, but Vistaprint has some really affordable options, and Vistaprint always has great deals and coupons. Get a nice table banner to go across your table and also a standing banner from Vistaprint. Little touches like that go a long way. It's the little touches and details that really wow people.

This is how you show up. It works the same way on social media. Make sure that you have nice, crisp graphics. Make sure that your pictures are always clear and that they're not grainy or distorted, so that you can always come across as a professional. I will go more in depth into branding in Part Two, but the take home is that the more serious you take yourself, the more serious other people will take you; so it's important that you stand up, show up, and show out.

Show up as the professional businesswoman that you are. Do not allow false humility to sneak in and make you act subservient to someone else just because you admire their work, or just because they've been in the business a little bit longer than you. Hold your composure, and always make sure that you show up and stand in your power.

9

The Secret to Getting What's Yours

"Be thankful for what you have; you'll end up having more. If you concentrate on what you don't have, you will never, ever have enough."
— Oprah Winfrey

The world is full of infinite possibilities, and it's time for you to step into your greatness and own your worth so you can get what's yours. As women, we are so used to giving away to so many people and making it a priority to get along with others and to be nice and be humble that after a while we don't even know how to get what belongs to us.

Has that ever happened to you? Have you ever been so busy celebrating somebody else's greatness, admiring someone else because they shine so brightly that that you forget to shine your own light?

Today we're going to break that cycle and we're going to send that mindset to the devil in hell because it is time for you to own your greatness so that you can get what's yours. We live in an abundant world. We live in a world full of possibilities. As a matter of fact, abundance is your birth-right. One of the universal laws of the world based on biblical principles, is the principle of life, more life, more abundantly. Your creator wanted you to experience more life so that you could bring more life into the world.

What is it that you can bring forth into the world where you can create more light? We live in a very dark place at times. A lot of people live lives centered around negativity, so how can you be that light, that force that shines through the world so that you can empower someone else to shine? Your gift was not given to you just to keep to yourself. In order to experience abundance, you have to be willing to let go and give more. If you have a beautiful talent, a wonderful skillset and a brilliant mind, then you are not serving the world by being shy and holding your talents all to yourself.

Once you become clear on what it is you were sent here to do you need to start sharing that purpose more, and more and more. Start serving, because the more you serve, the more you receive. As a matter of fact, when you look at the word "deserve" and you look at the art of creating income and generating revenue, money is simply an exchange of energy. It's an exchange of energy for value. If you are not earning the type of money that you want to earn, it means that you have not *deserved* it. In order for you to earn more money you have to be willing to serve more, because deserve is a derivative of Him. Him being a Creator, being God, being Universe, being Spirit, whatever you want to call him. I call him God, but whatever you want to call him, deserve means to be of service.

If you want to increase your income and you want to increase the amount of abundance that you experience, you need to serve more. No one is more deserving of anything than you are. There's no one out here who was created to be better than you. If someone has been blessed in an area, there is no reason why you cannot be blessed in that same area in your own unique way. If God has done it for one person, He can do it for you. You do not have to ever look at anyone else again from a place of lack or envy, because whatever they have is for them, and God has His own set of promises for you. If He did it for one, He can do it for you. That's the type of Creator we serve and abundant world that we live in.

Look at the world around you. Look at where you are now. You may be in your home, or you may be driving in your car. Look at the trees that are around you. Breathe in the air. Look at the birds. Think about the rivers and the oceans that flow. Think about the mountains and the valleys. Think about the lushness of the rainforest, and the trees and moss. Look at the creatures in the ocean. If all of these things can be created, why can't the type of success that you want to experience be created? There's no reason why it can't. We live in an abundant world where all you have to do is ask for what you want to receive. Believe it, and do the work that it takes in order to create those types of results.

There is a formula to success. You know what that the formula to success is? It's to follow the successful steps of someone else who is experiencing the same success that you want to experience. That's all you have to do, but you also have to believe that it can happen for you. If you do not believe that it can happen for you too, then it won't. You will repel it. The law of attraction is that like attracts like. Whatever thoughts that you produce will attract the same type of result.

Some people, like famed life coach Steve Chandler, refer to something similar called the Law of Creation. The Law of Creation states that you are given even more power because you're not just attracting results, but you are actually creating the type of results that you want to achieve. You are creating the type of life that you want to live and the type of relationships that you want to have. Step into your power and realize that you are a creator. You're not a victim. You are a warrior. You are a creator and you are a victor.

Now once you've digested all of this, the fact that you are a creator and that you have the power in your hands to manifest exactly what it is that you want, there is no reason that you cannot experience success. If you've ever felt like you couldn't achieve, you know it was a lie. Now you're ready to step into your power and own your worth. Because believe me, trust me, that thing that's in you, that desire, that flame that's in your heart, you didn't just create that flame. That flame didn't just appear in you. That was placed in you by your maker. That desire that you have, that's part of our spirit because we're not just physical beings, we're spirits living on this earth, and so that desire that you want can be achieved.

If there was no way for you to achieve your goal, that desire would have never been placed in you. That desire came from the Creator, so if the vision has been placed in you, provisions will be made for that vision. When a desire has been placed in you it is of God. Desire is derived from the meaning of the Father. If God has a placed a desire within you, that means that provisions will be made for that vision once you get clear, once you have an absolute resolve to achieve the thing that you want to achieve, and once you start taking those steps, that thing will happen for you.

Stay confident in who you are, and know that you are worth it, and you can achieve whatever it is that you envision.

10

Five Success Mindsets that Every Female Entrepreneur Needs

"In order to get to the next level of whatever you're doing, you must think and act in a wildly different way than you previously have been. You cannot get to the next phase of a project without a grander mind-set, more acceleration, and extra horsepower."

— Grant Cordone

More women than ever before are discovering that they have a gift that they could offer the world and the number of female entrepreneurs continues to be on the rise. Sadly, the numbers are also rising for women entrepreneurs who fail to make themselves a decent income. Entrepreneurship is not just about great ideas and skills. Building a successful company requires having a success mindset. Make sure that you have each one of these mindsets before you just quit.

You don't wait for the right time. In starting a business, there is no such thing as the "Right Time." Entrepreneurs are always prone to believing that the right time will come. Guess what? No matter how long you wait for it, it will never come. So regardless of where you are in your life right now, if you want to succeed, then start somewhere and start now.

You don't have to know it all. Entrepreneurs, especially women, often feel that they have to know everything before they can succeed as business persons. In fact, the most successful business owners do not have the answer to everything. So what do they have? They have the mindset that all of the knowledge that they need is out there for the taking. It may be on the internet, in a book, or with a mentor or peer – but the most important thing to remember is that if you do not know something, don't be too hard on yourself. The skills you need can be gained from experience and continuous practice. Eventually, you can also hire people who can help you in areas where you may be weak.

Don't let money get into your nerves. In other words, don't let money intimidate you. A lot of women entrepreneurs I know have grand dreams of earning six-figure incomes but when they reach that goal, they find that they can't handle their success. Why? Because they let money run them, instead of running the money. If the idea of handling $1 million scares you, then you might just find yourself sabotaging yourself and your business just to remain in your comfort zone. Remember, money is just a number.

You will run into setbacks. Be willing to make mistakes. As an entrepreneur, you are bound to have setbacks, failures and mistakes all throughout the life of your business. Don't let this run you down. Instead, focus on how you can make things better and how you can improve so that you can overcome your obstacles.

Your business is not all about you. You've heard this time and again, but let me give it to you straight: if you think you are the center of your business universe, then you are in big trouble. Focusing more on the benefits you will get from your business rather than what value it gives to your customers is a sure recipe for failure. Customers and clients can certainly tell if you are not providing them real value. The whole point of your business is to make your customer's lives better – focus on that first, and the money will follow.

Running your own enterprise is not a walk in the park. It is an exercise not only of your business prowess, but also of your character and personal growth. The sooner you make these mindset shifts, the sooner you can create a business that is thriving and viable. If you don't, then you might be passing up on the opportunities that can take you to greater heights – and that is certainly something you don't want to do

11

Three Reasons Why a Mastermind May be Right for You

"Surround yourself with people whose definition of you is not based on your history, but your destiny."
— TD Jakes

Purpose-driven adults are striving harder than ever to experience transformation, especially in business. Everyone has a goal. Whether it be a business goal or a personal goal, each one of us strives to be in the place that will bring us closer to the completion of that goal. Personally, being a part of a mastermind group has helped me greatly in achieving both my personal and business goals. I have never heard of a successful person who has not become a member of a mastermind group at some point in his life. I am such an advocate of masterminds that I have started running my own.

How does a mastermind work? A mastermind is a group of people meeting within a specific time frame (maybe weekly, monthly, even daily for some) to discuss challenges and problems together. It is a collaboration of like minds that gives you access to peer-to-peer mentoring, accountability and collaboration. If you like the idea of getting stuff done and not operating inside of a vacuum, then a mastermind would be perfect for you.

The concept of the mastermind pertains to a group of individuals with a common definitiveness of purpose working together in harmony to help each other achieve success. In his book, "Think and Grow Rich," Success Thought Leader Napoleon Hill wrote about something called a "mastermind alliance." He described a mastermind group as, "A friendly alliance with one or more persons who will encourage one to follow through with both plan and purpose. Every mind needs friendly contact with other minds, for food of expansion and growth." ~Napoleon Hill, "Master Key to Riches"

Here are 3 reasons why a mastermind might be right for you:

Knowledge Building Joining a mastermind not only allows its members to share their networks, but also gives them the opportunity to share their talents and knowledge in their respective areas of expertise. Each member of the mastermind group has a unique skill, experience and connections. Through active interactions within the group, you will find that you are able to offer solutions and get solutions for the challenges you are currently facing. You are also able to get tips and strategies, which serve as your shortcut to finding the right solution. In my private mastermind there is an emphasis on branding, podcasting and creating revenue. Being a part of a mastermind also opens you the opportunity of hearing what has worked for others, as well as what did not work for them so that you learn from their experiences.

Networking A mastermind group allows you to expand your network exponentially. Joining a mastermind gives you access to the network of the members of your group and this can also lead to you finding someone within the group that is a perfect fit for you to work or collaborate with and vice versa.

You also have the chance to get promoted within the network of your group members and you can also find ways to help each other through cross promotion. I can attest that joining a mastermind group has allowed me to double my current network of connections, which in turn gave me access to more prospects and leads for my business. Being in a network of like-minded peeps also helped me to bust through mindset barriers and limiting beliefs that I never would've been able to conquer on my own.

Exclusivity A mastermind group or program makes you part of an exclusive community. Before becoming part of a mastermind group, you go through a rigorous application process where members are screened to see if they are the right fit. This is done because of the notion that each member has a mutual need for the benefits that each member can bring to the group. In a mastermind group, you invest in helping each other succeed. You help each other conquer your fears and hurdle through obstacles and the value of these relationships formed are priceless. Another important aspect of being part of a mastermind is that it gives you accountability partners so you can accomplish what you set out to achieve. Sometimes, life can easily sidetrack us, but knowing that you have a group or mentor that holds you accountable helps keep you focused and engaged.

Joining a mastermind is one of the best things you can do to work toward the achievement of your goals. This group will be there to support you, give you the best advice and share with you their expert knowledge. If you would like to join a supportive group that is centered on positive entrepreneurs who are committed to living with purpose and prosperity, join my free group at _http://brandybutleronline.com/community._

12

Three Things to Do Before You Quit

"You were born to win, but to be a winner you must plan to win, prepare to win, and expect to win."
— Zig Ziglar

Now that you're clear on what you want, you've named your treasure, done your research and gotten in the right mindset, you probably feel like you're ready to just quit. I've been in those shoes, where I felt stuck, where I just wanted to quit. I've been in that place where I've wanted to quit and I felt like my job was holding me back from growing my brand.

But one thing that I love to tell people about the Girl Just Quit brand is that, I am not telling anyone to just up and quit their job. Let's be clear about that. Don't go around quitting your job and then coming back telling me, "Brandy, I quit. Loan me $100." It's not going to happen. I'm not just telling you to leave all willy-nilly and be impulsive. There should be some strategy around your decision and that's why in this chapter, we're going to discuss three things that you must do before you quit your job.

Inner Work - Identification. You have to do this work first. This is so important. This has to be the foundation of your work because if you don't recognize this, you'll end up making the same mistake over and over again. Get clear on why you hate your job. What is it about your job that you truly hate? Is it the current role that you fill? Do you feel unfulfilled with the work that you do at your current employer? Do you just hate the role? Do you hate the skills that you have to use day-to-day? Or is it the environment? Is it the team you're on? Would you be happier if you were on another team? Would you be happier if you were at the same employer but you were in a different role?

You need to get clear on those types of things because if that's the case, those things could be relatively easy to fix. If you find that these things are true, you can just move to another team. You could maybe move to another department. Ask yourself, "Am I really happy with my current employer? Could I be happy doing some other type of work at this particular job?" If you're unclear about that, think about the role that you fill right now and the line of work that you are in. Would you be happy doing that same job at another employer? Sometimes it's as simple as being dissatisfied with company culture. Sometimes you're at a job and the company culture just does not align with your personal beliefs, your core values and your personality. Sometimes you could find happiness in your work by leaving that environment all together. It takes some work such as applying and interviewing at different companies, but get clear on it. Could you be happy doing the type of work that you do now at another company?

Or are you just ready for a career switch, period? Has your time run out doing that role and that line of work that you do regardless of the company that you work for? That is I went through during the last part of my IT career. When I was moving around from job to job I would feel like, "Okay, this is a new opportunity, new energy." The honeymoon phase would be great but after the honeymoon wore off, I was back at that same place of feeling stuck and not wanting to be there because my time in that career field was just over. I went into that career, like many of us, right out of college and picked a career for the cash, for the moo-la, and after a while I just outgrew that career, period.

I really want you to get clear as you plot out the next steps toward your career and for your life, especially if you're 30-plus. Time is of the essence and it goes by faster and faster. You can't get back time. It's our most valuable commodity. Get clear on exactly what it is that you hate about your job so that you don't repeat the same mistakes by jumping into the next career or the next company. Don't just try some quick fix. Really get to the root of the problem that you're having in your career right now.

You're going to need to do a lot of work to figure that out. Get a journal and write down how you feel. Start journaling this activity. Write out some adjectives about yourself. Describe yourself, and then think about the way that you feel about yourself and your description. Are you showing up like that at your job? Likewise, is your job showing up like that for you? Doing this can help figure out the misalignment.

Gain clarity about what it is that you really want to do. We discussed this in chapter three, but this is so important that it needs to be repeated. Make sure you are clear. If for whatever reason, some of the self-reflection, self-inventory and feedback of friends is not working, then get a coach. Don't stay stuck. Time is of the essence. You don't have time to waste. Get a coach if you're having difficulty gaining that clarity.

Save some money. This is huge because you see so many people on the internet after leaving their jobs saying, "I love my new career and within three months I had a $30,000 launch and I was making six figures." This may not happen for you, so while you're still on your job, save some money for your dream. If you're at that point where you're saying, "You know what? I am going to eventually leave my job. I'm going to pursue my passion and my purpose and I'm going to build my platform or my organization," make sure that you save for it while you're at work. Your job is your investor. It may sound cliché, but it is. You have more opportunities to build your brand, to pour into your brand, and to invest in yourself while you're working than if you just left your job cold turkey without any income coming in.

That isn't a good place to be. It's hard. It's rough. Do I think that the universe does some amazing things? YES. Do I think that God makes provision for vision? I absolutely do. However, there are some things that you could do in an intelligent, thought-out, planned-out fashion, and saving the money and investing in your brand while you work is one of the smartest things that you can do.

It takes a lot of time and energy to grow a brand. Depending on what industry you're in, you might need to travel to conferences. You'll need to invest in a website. You need to invest in classes, courses, coaching and the mindset development to get the skills that you need.

You don't need to just haul off and quit your job. That may work for some people but it won't work for all. If you have the option, try to be strategic with your job transition. Gain some exit strategies. Get some mentoring. Read some books. Get some training. Invest into your brand while you work and gain some clients and customers while you're already working so that you can already be building profits and revenue while you have a secure job in place. This will enable you to test out your business concept prior to you "burning the ship".

I'm not trying to completely discourage someone who is ready to just burn a bridge and say, "I'm gone! I'm quitting! F this job!" If you're a trailblazer like that, I wish you much success. However, if you're someone who has a bit of risk aversion and is a little bit unsure, try working on your strategy for leaving while you work.

13

Three Simple Ways to Get In Action

"When your clarity meets your conviction and you apply action to the equation, your world will begin to transform before your eyes."
— Lisa Nichols

Here are my top three ways for you to get yourself in action so that you can gain momentum for your brand.

Number One is simple. Start where you are. Don't wait until you get the fancy camera. I know you probably want that T5I or whatever Canon camera that's $600, $700 or $800. Stop it. Start where you are. If you want to start doing videos, use your cell phone. The camera is pretty decent. Get a nice app. You can start making videos now. If you want to start blogging, just start. Go get a wordpress.org blog. Start writing articles. Boom! Now you have a blog. Stop waiting to get more money for a top-of-the-line website. Stop telling yourself, "when I lose weight I'll start doing videos." Start now, where you are today, with whatever resources you have. Imperfect action is better than no action. You can always course correct, but you can't learn or get anywhere if you're not doing anything. When you take action, you will start to attract the resources that you need and they will manifest in your life.

Number Two: Make a bold declaration of what it is that you're going to do. Sometimes we just need that accountability. If you know that you really want to do something, get bold now. Write it on Facebook. Tell people "Today, I'm writing my book." I did that when I was writing this. I told people, "I'm writing my book. My book is going to release this year. I'm not going to fail. I'm going to back up my word." I challenge you to do the same thing. If you've been playing with that idea in your mind for a long time, you need some checks and balances in your life. Tell people what it is that you're going to do and mentally you're not going to want to tell a lie. You're going to want to keep your word. Having public accountability is a great way for you to follow through with that thing that you want to do and that you tell people that you're going to do. Make a bold declaration so that you can get that thing done.

Number Three: If you're still stuck after you've started where you are and made your bold declaration, but you still don't feel like you are in action enough, or you feel like there's something more that you can be doing, get a coach. A coach or a mentor will push you because all of us have blind spots and sometimes we just aren't aware of them. When you're the picture in the frame, you can't see what's inside the frame. You're boxed in. You need someone else to push you into your greatness so that you can accomplish those goals that you want to achieve. Also a coach or a mentor has already been through this before. They can help you to shortcut through some of those road blocks.

Mentors are often free. If you're blessed enough to have a great mentor in your life, do whatever it is that they tell you to do. Actually implement the advice that they give you. But if you don't have access to a mentor, all is not lost. Read books by some of your favorite mentors. Maybe you really look up to Oprah or Deepak Choprah. You can start implementing the lessons that they have in their books or their videos.

Still, you'll get faster results if you're actually working one on one with someone who can actually peer into your brand and business concept to give you the guidance that you need to move forward.

If you are a high performing woman who is ready to work with a coach, I invite you to apply for a complimentary breakthrough session with me: *http://brandybutleronline.com/breakthrough*.

PART II: FROM MINDSET TO MONEY; THE PRACTICAL STEPS TO RUNNING YOUR BUSINESS

14

Why Momentum Is More Important Than Money

"I've found that luck is quite predictable. If you want more luck, take more chances, be more active, show up more often."

— Brian Tracy

In this chapter I'm going to talk to you about the power of momentum. Initially, you need to be more focused on momentum than you are money. The reason being is that the momentum is going to bring the money.

I have to tell you about this because I see one problem with so many female entrepreneurs: perfection paralysis. This is the issue that arises when someone is not taking an action because they hide behind the facade of perfection which really is just another form of procrastination. You have to get out into the world. You have to bring your work forth. You cannot leave all of your work bottled up inside of you. Your ideas are no good until they are manifested. Once they are manifested, you can tweak and get them to the next level, but while all of your ideas are in your head you cannot create any impact on yourself, on your business, or the people you were sent here to serve.

You want to go ahead and take an action. I don't care if you make a mistake. I don't care if it's not perfect. You have to get it in action. Imperfect action brings perfect momentum and through the process of just doing, you will get better.

Let's say that you're a bootstrapped entrepreneur and you don't initially want to spend a lot of money on a graphic designer or a web designer. Don't let the lack, or what you perceive as a lack, stop your momentum. Don't let the limited resources keep you from getting a project out. You've got to get the website up so maybe you start off with a DIY site and put it up. Now, is your site going to look like you're a guru mentor or who has spent $5,000, $15,000 or $20,000 on their website? No it's not, but it's a start and a way for you to let the world know who you are. It's a place for you to create a professional brand, turn your website into an automated cash machine and start creating the money you need to eventually upgrade the website.

Another example: You want to do your first virtual event so that you can bring in some clients. You create a webinar but you can't use the expensive high-level technology. That's fine. Go find something that you can afford or use a free 30-day trial for a while and see how you like it. During that 30 days come up with a program to create the money so that you can afford it.

You have to get into momentum. You have to get in action so that you can interact with your audience and bring forth the value that you are supposed to bring to impact your bottom line. You cannot get stuck in not being ready. At some point you have to be ready enough because your ready enough may be someone else's ready. Your ready enough may be your 80% but your 80% may be someone else's 100%. Create the momentum and when you have momentum you have to be intentional about keeping it.

Let's say that you stumble along the way or have a disappointment. Maybe you created a free opt-in, some type of lead generation, and you're trying to get a lot of people on your email list. You wanted to gain 500 new people on your email list and you only got 100. Well, you can't sulk about that. You can't cry and belittle yourself and beat yourself up for it. You've got to pick up and move on to the next task because once you stop the momentum, it stalls and it takes so much effort to build it back up.

The momentum is the steam. It's the inertia. You have to keep moving and keep the steam going so that at some point you can eventually bubble up. Think of a boiling pot, it eventually steams and then it bubbles up. You want that bubble up effect from putting all of these ingredients in your pot. You've had online and off-line events. You have clients and customers. You have testimonials. You see how all of this builds up over time; each different piece and ingredient. It builds up.

Then you have your first speaking event and then your second, your third and fourth. Now you're getting paid for speaking. All of these are different ingredients are in your pot for success and you have to keep going so you can keep up the momentum so that the people that are watching can eventually know that you are the person that they *have* to work with because they know that you're the person who's going to help them solve their problem.

Maybe there is a brand or a company that you want to work with. You have to keep the momentum going so that they can say, "Wow, she's done this project. Look at her body of work. This lady is serious about her business. She's a great representation of her brand. This is in total alignment with our company's core values. We think that she would be a valuable asset and we want to move forward with signing the contract or creating this proposal." You've built up your momentum enough to get the company's eyes on the brand.

You've created a brand that's sticky and smoking hot. Now you have major influencers that are digging what it is that you bring to the world. They like your vibe and you're the go-to girl that everybody wants to connect with. People want to partner with you because you have a great spirit. If you have great energy and great content people will be drawn to you and will want to pair up with you. You could even attract angel investors or someone who is looking to pour into someone else's business. You've kept yourself on their radar, you have stayed in action, you have worked through all of your imperfections, you have created the type of visibility for yourself as a magnetic brand and people want to do business with you, they want to connect with you. They want to be served by you. They want to partner with you.

Stay in action. Get off the sideline. It's fine if you look at Periscope and YouTube or you watch other people's brands and get on other brands' email lists, but while you're watching don't forget to execute and create your own imperfect action.

15

Money Matters. What Do You Need to Replace Your Salary?

"Your income can grow only to the extent that you do."
— T. Harv Eker

How much money do you need in order to quit?

As a female entrepreneur, I know how important it is to be able to have revenue in order to pay your bills, pay the mortgage, buy the groceries and do whatever it takes to take care of your kids. If you're wondering, or you're wishing, about replacing your job salary with your business revenue, then, while you do have an employer and are on this journey to create this dream business, I want you to get real about your numbers. Ask yourself "How much money do I need in order to replace my job salary?"

Let's say that you make $75,000 annually. That breaks down to a little bit over $6,000 per month before you take out Uncle Sam's cut, leaving roughly $5,100 per month. With insurance, health benefits, 401K, and all of that good stuff, let's just round it off and say that you need at least $5,000 per month in order to replace your job salary and be at the same level that you're at with your job.

While you're on the job you need to get very clear about what you are going to do to generate this $5,000 per month. Before you get to this point, however, you need to be clear about what your products or services are.

You've identified your "why" and the types of products and services that you can offer. Now you know that you need to bring in $5,000 per month and you know what you want to be, either a business consultant or a coach.

Now you can make decisions. You can say, "I need to bring in at least five clients per month that pay me $1,000 per month," or, "I really don't want to deal with a lot of people. I don't want to have a high volume of customers and clients that I'm dealing with on a monthly basis, so maybe I'll offer two VIPs or two bigger ticket packages for $2,500," or maybe you just shoot for having one client per month that pays you $5,000.

You may wonder what you are even going to offer for $5,000 per month, let alone $1,000 per month. I don't know what that looks like for you, but what I want you to know is that we live in an abundant world, and there are people who are willing to buy your products and services and knowledge. They are willing to invest in the skills and the services that you bring; you just have to figure out who those people are.

Maybe they are business-to-business clients, meaning another business person like you. Maybe you are marketing to the old you back when you were going through a hurdle that you've already crossed, and you want to make life easier for yourself. Maybe you don't even want to deal with the consumer marketplace because, honey, they can't pay you enough coins, or you're at a point where you don't want to just replace your work salary first year out. You want to exceed it.

Maybe you want to go after corporate contracts. Maybe you want to go after sponsorships. These are things that you need to be identifying while you are blessed with the job that you have now. No matter if you hate the job or not, even if you feel like it's a soul-sucking job, while you have that cushion and the ability to maneuver around, get clear on the amount of money that you want to bring in once you leave your job. Once you're clear on the amount of money that you want to bring in, then you can be clear on how you're going to go about getting it.

Now you need to take three steps toward actually marketing your business to get the money.

Number One: Get into the habit of marketing your business while you're at work. I know that you may feel like you're already strapped with the money that you have now, but imagine yourself being even more strapped when you don't have the cushion of having a job; You should be using at least 20% of your budget towards marketing, so you need to figure out how you can market your business now? Can you advertise on some popular blogs? Can you invest in Facebook ads? You absolutely have to be marketing your business. Otherwise, you're not going to get any momentum; so identify how you can be marketing your business right now.

Number Two: Get out and mingle. Go local. There's a huge world outside of online marketing, and there are so many opportunities right in your own city. How can you get out and mix and mingle and represent yourself as the businesswoman you are? I don't care how big your business is or even if your business hasn't even fully launched. Go get some business cards. I love MOO business cards, because the card stock quality is just amazing. They're nice and big, and you can get so many trendy, custom designs, and it's a nice, heavy card, so it gives you a great first impression.

After you get your business cards, go out mix and mingle in your city. You will be surprised who you meet. You may meet some potential clients. You may meet a new sponsor; you may meet an angel investor. You never know who you might meet, but you've got to get out from behind the computer and mix and mingle in your city.

Number Three: Be bold and let people know what you bring to the world. People are often scared to say what they're doing on their personal profiles on social media, or to their family and friends. You have to tell people what it is that you do in order for them to know that you're an option to help solve the problem that they have.

Sometimes, we get so stuck in ourselves, and we think that it's apparent to everyone what we do, when actually, we have not done a good job of marketing ourselves. People don't know who you are. They don't know that you have a business. In your head you have a business, but nobody else knows. Therefore, you don't have customers. Get bold about letting people know what you do. Be able to say: "Hey, I consult. I facilitate workshops. I have a virtual assistant business."

Whatever it is that you do, be bold about posting it on social media, on your personal site, on your personal profile, on your business profile and to family and friends. Ask your friends to let people know that you offer services in a particular area.

Be bold about your offerings, market your business, advertise and get out and mix and mingle locally. Start participating in these activities now, before you leave your job.

16

Five Ways to Raise Funds for Your Small Business

"When you have a desire and it's coupled with a sense of urgency, the Law of Polarity states that the way to fulfill that desire must also be present and possible."

— David Neagle

You have a dream in your heart, you KNOW that you were meant to do more in the world and now you are ready to enter the global marketplace and start your own business. The problem is that you weren't born with a silver spoon in your mouth. You have the drive and the skill, however you don't necessarily have the financial backing that you need. Perhaps you've maxed your credit cards, dipped into your 401K and exhausted every last friggin' resource easily available to you. Your business concept is solid, but you are in need of a cash infusion to take you to that next level. This is the life of a startup entrepreneur and many of us are there or have been there before. So, how do you generate funding for your business in today's day and age when the traditional banking system seems to have more stringent guidelines than ever?

Self-Investment This is also called bootstrapping. Initially you will have to find some way to invest your own money into your dream. Whether it's credit cards, dipping into savings, etc. People need to see that you have a viable business concept before they will be willing to invest their money with you. Your personal money and sweat equity is a prerequisite to any external business validation and contribution. This is called having "Skin in the Game."

Family and Friends Are you able to get a 0% loan from any of your family and friends? For some people this is not an option. However, if you do receive a small business loan from someone in your personal circle, give your loved ones reassurance that you will repay their loan. Keep it professional and create a promissory note that reflects the terms of the agreement.

Business Partner You've heard the saying "teamwork makes the dream work," or perhaps "two wallets are better than one." It is usually easier to generate funds when there is more than one party involved. However, having a partnership brings its own unique set of challenges such as balance of partner roles, effort, clear terms, etc.

Crowdfunding The digital world has made it possible for projects, causes and business owners to generate funds online from a large group of funders in a fast and efficient way. There are two types of crowdfunding:

- **Rewards Based** – Funders either give donations or purchase products or services as a pre-sell. This is highly effective for businesses to validate their idea and reach new customers. Kickstarter is a good example.

- **Equity Based** brings investors in your company in the form of equity or debt. Funders become an investor/ shareholder in your company. Crowd Funder is an example of an equity based crowdfunding platform.

Microloans If none of the other options seem like a match for your situation, I encourage you to try a resource that I'm currently using, Kiva Zip. Kiva Zip uses an entrepreneur's network as a measure of creditworthiness. Borrowers invite family and friends to start their fundraising. After reaching a designated threshold, the Kiva Zip community takes care of the rest. It's a simple, transparent way to help small businesses.

What I love about Kiva is the fact that it provides 0% interest loans up to $5,000 for small businesses and entrepreneurs who are financially excluded and underserved. Roughly 90% of the campaigns reach their goal and are funded within 60 days or less. For every new lender that a borrower invites to Kiva, the organization matches several of the contributions dollar for dollar. Additionally, if you bring 45 new lenders on board, Kiva will match any of your following campaign contributions dollar for dollar up to $500.

Remember, your current financial state does not have to prevent you from living your dream. Thinking that you don't have the money is merely an excuse. There are all type of options available for the tenacious entrepreneur who is willing to bust her hump, hustle and fight for her dream.

17

How to Get Support with Your Business

"As long as you are alive, you will either live to accomplish your own goals and dreams or be used as a resource to accomplish someone else's."
— Grant Cordone

As entrepreneurs we face so many obstacles and challenges. Some of them are financial, some are mental, and some are just the result of not having a support system from family and friends. As entrepreneurs, we're visionaries. God has placed a vision in us and we see it so clearly that we can nearly touch it. We can smell it. We can almost feel it. But it can get very difficult when you believe in something and the people who are closest to you don't get it and don't see it.

Lord knows, don't try anything that's innovative or has anything with tech, then they really don't get it. Especially if you didn't come from a family or a background that is used to the entrepreneurial or technology mindset. It's a very lonely feeling when you see something that's caught your eye. You think you can do it. You've been following different mentors and researching. But it becomes very hard when you see a reality for yourself and there's no one near you living out that reality. You want to do something innovative. You see examples online or on TV of people doing this thing that you want to do, but there's no one in your circle doing it. You can start to feel like it's just a dream.

When you have a vision you need to meditate on a regular basis. It helps you to get centered. It helps you to increase your faith. Get in your quiet zone so that you can hear and process the different visions that are coming to you, because that's your internal compass. That's your set of navigation within you. You can really tap into that and harness it by meditating. You want to definitely work on your faith and your meditation because you're going to have dark times and times when all you'll be able to depend on is yourself. You're going to have to trust your gut and your instinct, and meditation will help you do that.

Create the time on a regular basis to meditate. That may be 15 minutes for you each morning, or 30 minutes or an hour. Make sure that you get into your quiet spot and take time to just think about how you want your business to look. That's why vision boards are so important, especially early on in your journey. Refer to your vision board often. Dream big. Meditate on that vision.

I have learned to trust my gut and my instincts, and not only is this important, it can be life-saving....

I was 36 weeks pregnant and just one week away from my scheduled C-section with our third child. Because this was my third pregnancy, there was no need for me to wait all the way to 40 weeks when I was going to have to get a C-section again anyway. Things had been going well except for the fact that I had a pain shooting through my back all of a sudden. I had this pain that was shooting through my back into my pelvis. It didn't feel normal. I couldn't lay on my side, I couldn't get comfortable.

I had just left my scheduled OBGYN appointment the day before and everything checked out fine, but by that evening I was in pain. I told my husband, "This isn't right." He tried to calm me down because sometimes he feels as if I'm a hypochondriac or over exaggerate, but I knew that things were not right. I called my doctor and she told me to come right in. We went in but as luck would have it, right when we went into the doctor's office, she had been called in to deliver another baby, so we had to see one of the other doctors, a younger doctor.

She told me what I was experiencing was endo-skeletal pain. I told her, "This is not endo-skeletal pain. This is not muscular pain. This pain is not right." She told me, "Take 2 aspirin and take a nap." I told her, "This is not right. I know I shouldn't be experiencing this pain." But she insisted that as long as I took two ibuprofen and a nap, the pain would subside. We left the doctor's office pissed. My husband tried to calm me down. But I knew this was not right.

I continued to toss and turn throughout the night and tried to get the rest that I needed, but the pain was killing me. My mother told me, "If that pain keeps going, you go to the doctor, and I mean tonight." But my husband kept telling me, "You're going to be okay, it's okay. The doctor would have told you if anything was wrong." However, at some point in your life, you need to know how to trust your instinct and my instinct was telling me this wasn't right. So I called my doctor and she told me to go to the hospital.

When I got to the hospital, my pain level was probably about a seven on a 10-point scale, and I wasn't having contractions, but they told me that as a precaution, because I had already had two C-sections before, that they were going to go ahead and schedule the surgery, because they didn't want me at risk for a uterine rupture. When my doctor got there and they began the C-section, she told me, "Brandy, I am so glad that you came in, that you listened to your intuition and that you trusted your instinct, because if you would have waited any longer, you would have had a uterine rupture. Your uterus was so thin that I could have delivered your baby by plucking your uterus with my finger." You see, my uterus was starting to tear at the incision from my previous two births. The only thing that was holding my baby in was my bladder.

God has entrusted each and every one of us with instinct, and no matter what, no matter how crazy you may sound to the experts, no matter how crazy your spouse, your mate, your family and your friends may think you are, at some point you have to be willing to be crazy enough to trust yourself. You have to have the fortitude to trust your instinct, and this will relate to various aspects of your life; your job, your friends, your relationships and the different decisions you have to make. Listen to your gut. It will not steer you wrong and, at some point, trusting your instinct maybe be the very thing that saves your life.

Now back to the chapter...The next thing that you need to do is know that it's not your family's responsibility to support your vision. God didn't give that vision to them. He gave it to you. If he gave your vision to everyone else, everyone else would be doing it. There's a reason and a purpose that he gave that vision to you. If you don't believe in God, you may want to call it a higher spirit, or the universe. But whatever you call it, there's a reason why that vision was given to you. God placed that vision in you for you to carry that vision out. He wants you to do it. He didn't want your mama to do it, because if he wanted her to do it, he would've given the vision to her.

You may be misunderstood. Other people may not get it. The best thing that you can do is walk boldly and keep going. You can keep pushing and you can make it happen. Then, once you start to experience small successes and small wins, it will become easier for other people to buy into the vision. Once they can see the progress, you'll be able to get more of their support.

I'm going to keep it honest with you. I'm going to keep it 100. Some people may not ever get what you're doing. They may not ever buy into your vision. You may have some family members who are sarcastic, and that's just the way they are. My father is that way. He's just sarcastic. He's always been that way, so I know that there are certain things that I can get from him when it comes to my business, and there are some things that we just can't discuss.

Don't entrust a conversation about your vision with a dream killer, a negative Nelly or a dream zapper. You have to protect your vision from vampires. Know who you can and can't talk to about your vision. For instance, you may have a girlfriend who's thriving in corporate America and moving up the ranks. All she can see is her paycheck. She may not get why you would want to risk your finances or risk your livelihood. Why you would want to take on such a risk? She may not understand.

When you first decide on this vision or this goal, you may share it with everyone because you're excited. But I want you to watch them as they process the conversation that you're having. Take note of who is really for you and who is against you. Protect your dream. You cannot discuss your dream and your plans with everyone because some people are energy vampires. You have to protect your vision like it's your baby because it is. You're going to have to nurture your vision in your womb until it's birthed. But once that vision is birthed, it's still a baby.

Think about newborn babies. When you first have a baby, the baby can't hold his head up on his own. You have to support a baby's neck. After a while, that baby gets stronger and can hold his own head up. A baby can't walk at first, he has to crawl. Then he starts to walk, but he's still wobbly at first. You get scared every time the baby goes around corners. You're scared the baby is going to fall and hit his head.

Your business is the same way. Your vision is the same way. It's going to be wobbly at first. You don't want to expose all of your plans and all of your big dreams to someone who might harm your baby. You want to be deliberate about finding circles of like-minded people who are having the same experiences that you're having and get where you're coming from. Back in the day, people would find forums. These days there are still some forums out there, but for the most part, people are engaging in Facebook groups. Find a forum or a Facebook group that has the same type of goals and pursuits that you're after at the moment. That's a great way to find the support you need, because it doesn't matter if the group is virtual, you just need someone to let you know that it can be done.

To recap:
- Find a support system either online or offline.
- Find a mentor or a coach to give you the support you need.
- Be your own cheerleader and believe that you can do it. Understand that you have everything you need to get it done.
- Protect your vision from energy vampires.
- Find a like-minded community of people.

The steps outlined are not only how you experience success, but get support. It takes a village to grow a vision. The more support that you have, the more successful you'll become.

18

The Definition of a Brand

"Your number-one job is to tell your story to the consumer wherever they are, and preferably at the moment they are deciding to make a purchase."
— Gary Vaynerchuk

What exactly does it mean to be a brand?

The first thing that I want you to know is that you are your brand. No matter where you are and no matter what you're doing, you are a reflection of your brand. Your brand is not just a website or a logo. Your brand is you.

Before I dive into this subject too far, let's discuss what it means to be a brand. By definition, a brand is a type of product, manufactured by a particular company under a particular name. A brand is also defined as a particular identity or image regarded as an asset. The most important thing that I want you to know is that, as a brand, as an individual, as a person that was created by a higher power, you were created from something greater than you. You're an asset to the world: your skills, your wisdom and the value that you bring.

You are an asset wherever you go and with the work that you do or will do in the marketplace. The whole purpose of having a superstar brand mindset is to help you to move into a state of mind where you are charging for the work and the value that you are bringing along with it; that you are doing whatever is necessary to be competitive in the market place; that you can gain a visibility that you need as an artist to grow your brand. Know that you're an asset. Understand that throughout these years of your life, you have acquired a unique skillset and experience that will help you to serve others.

That's one of the most important things about being a brand: knowing that you're an asset. You have worth. Own your worth. Again, your brand is not just a logo. It's not just your website. Yes, those things are extremely important because they're a reflection of you. Your visual representation is a reflection on how much people will perceive the value that they'll get from you. People won't necessarily want to pay high prices for your work if your marketing collateral is weak and it looks very DIY-boot-leggish. Make sure that you are striving to look your very best, no matter what your budget point.

If there is something with your branding that is a bit off or it doesn't look as polished and professional as it could be, because you built it with your own hands, then be willing to outsource that to someone else. Do what you can in order to have your brand reflect you as well as possible so that you can illustrate to the world the level of quality and service that comes along with doing business with you.

The next thing we're going to discuss is your brand style. Your brand style is basically the essence of who you are as a human being. Your brand style has a lot to do with your own personal style and personality. Who are you as a person? What are some of your strengths and interests? Those are the things that you should be leading with as you build this business because you want this to be a business that you can be excited about.

Your brand style is going to be the way that you communicate with people. It's going to be the way that your brand looks visually.

All of those things are a part of your brand's communication, whether it's verbal communication or visual communication. This communication, your brand style, is going to be what helps people to connect and resonate with you.

I always knew the importance of branding, even with my first business and even though it started out as a hobby. I knew it was very important for me to give the customer an experience, because they weren't walking into a physical store. The only way that I could really give them a great personal experience was by giving them superior packaging. I made sure that I shipped all of my jewelry in a pink jewelry box with a zebra ribbon. I would ship my t-shirts in little cinched, zebra-patterned satchels. In addition, I always included a thank you card from me and my husband thanking the customer for supporting our business.

Just by going the extra mile with the packaging, customers were excited to get their packages in the mail because it would be like opening a gift when they received it. The result was that I got a lot of repeat customers and people loved to take pictures of my products and tag me and post them to my page. It was awesome.

Even though my business took off fast, I made sure that I invested in myself. I was always trying to learn how to make my jewelry business different. I was always working on a unique skill. Especially as a minority woman, I always try to do something more technical. This is a good lesson for any niche that you're in. You always want to have a "purple cow," meaning that you always want to find some type of way to make your business different and to stand out.

You always want to be aware of what's popular and current trends, but you also want to make sure that there's something about you that distinguishes you from everyone else. With me, it was my packaging; it was my branding; it was the skills that

I would bring to the jewelry making. All of that helped to grow that business and then I learned the power of leveraging influences.

Now, the foundation of your brand is the message. If you don't have a message that's worthwhile and has substance, it is going to be hard to monetize your message. You need to understand what that message is. I'm going to be honest with you upfront. You may not know what your message is yet. Honestly, that message may change from time to time, and that's okay. Give yourself the grace to know that you're starting with what you have and that you're going to refine your message. You're going to course correct later, but you have to just get started.

Something that you can do in order to refine your message on your own is journal. Journaling helps you to get clarity. It helps you to write out your thoughts and get those creative juices going. Take some time to write out some answers to the following questions:

- Who are you?
- What is the message that you want to share with the world? Be your own cheerleader and believe that you can do it. Understand that you have everything you need to get it done.
- What is it that you really want someone else to know?
- What is your bio?
- How do you want people to describe you?
- If you were called to be in a major publication today, how would you want the publication to describe you?

All of these questions are tied to your message. If you are not clear about what your message is just yet, try writing a message to the old you. Send yourself a message that solves a problem that you used to deal with. Perhaps you want to help the old version of you, or someone like yourself. Maybe you want to help someone to leap over a hurdle that you used to experience in your own life. That's what happened to me. That was the inspiration behind my brand Girl Just Quit. I wanted to be able to help other women to own their purpose and figure out how they could live a life filled with purposeful work where they would be able to create revenue in order to replace jobs that they were no longer happy with.

Or maybe you want to speak to the future you. Maybe you want to speak to an aspiration that you have. It may be something that you're extremely interested in and maybe you're not at that particular level yet, but you're speaking to where you are going. There are a lot of different ways that you can help people through your brand by being in the position to help solve a problem that you used to have. Or you can help yourself by speaking about working toward an aspiration of yours.

You will be able to generate money from anything you work toward. I want you to really focus on what it is that's really tied to your core. What's your life's work? This is the business that I suggest that you focus on throughout this book. The things that I've taught you in this book, you'll be able to apply to any brand. Maybe you want to just have a fun brand for the moment. It might not be your lifelong work. I still urge you to really get centered and to truly understand what it is that moves you. Even if it isn't this particular brand, the next brand that you build can be something substantial; something very close to your "WHY" and to your core.

19

The Brand Experience

"Developing your personal brand is key to monetizing your passion online."

— Gary Vanyerchuk

Let's discuss your brand experience because this is more important than how the brand looks. The experience is tied to some of the work discussed in brand archetypes. The Brand Archetype theory is linked to Maslow's psychology theory. The archetypes intuitively correspond with your personality. If you'd like more information about which brand archetype your personality matches best, I suggest that you research this subject online. I think you'll find this topic quite interesting.

When you think about your brand experience, how do you want to make people to feel about your brand?

When people come in contact with your brand, when they see you on social media, when you've put up a post, whether it be on your personal page or your business page or on Instagram, how do you want to make people feel? Do you want people to feel like you have a very professional brand, one that's very factually based? Do you want people to feel like you're a leader? Do you want people to feel like your brand is warm, like they know you like they're your friend? Do you want people to feel like you are accessible, like you're a regular old guy or girl?

All of these different feelings and experiences go back to the brand archetype, because if you can understand your brand archetype, you can understand how to assign your brand to a certain genre. Then you can understand the different wording in communications that you're branding and your social media status updates, your blog posts and your Periscope videos. You'll understand what type of messaging and communication you should be having with your audience.

Once you understand the brand archetype that you align with, you will also better understand the experience that you want people to have when they come into contact with your brand, do you want people to feel like you're snarky? Do you have a level of sarcasm and you want people to know that about you? Own that. Whatever it is, own it, so that you'll know how to play up that experience, because the experience and the energy is everything when you're building a brand that's irresistible.

When you can play up that experience that you know that you want your customer to have, you're able to resonate that much deeper with them. I want you to take this time out to think about the experience that you want people to have when they interact with your brand. Think about the experience that you want them to have in real life and also virtually. If you decide to conduct business locally or you do workshops or whatever you may decide, what's the experience that you want associated with your brand?

If you're going to do virtual workshops or virtual trainings and webinars or videos, what's the experience that you want the person on the other end of the screen to have? Think about your brand experience because all of that ties into your brand style. If you can understand how your personality strengths align best with your brand archetype, then you'll be that much more positioned to show up more powerfully.

20

Three Ways to Get People to Pay Attention to Your Brand

"Rich people are willing to promote themselves and their value. Poor people think negatively about selling and promotion."
— T Hary Ecker

In the beginning when it comes to your brand visibility, things feel so quiet that you can actually hear the damn crickets feverishly whisking and rubbing their legs back and forth, back and forth. You wonder "When is it going to be my time, when will people notice my work?" I remember a time when I felt so freaking invisible. I would host events or speak publicly and only seven people would show up. UNDERSTAND that four out of seven of the people were related to me. Talk about underwhelming! SO… what changed between last year and now? Well, quite a few things, mindset being one of the primary factors. However, I'll share with you how I've truly been able to get people to not only pay attention to me, but take action as well.

Stick with it

So what if only a few people like your social media statuses or show up for your events. Persistence and consistency show people that you are in it to win it. *Baybeee* let me tell you, you can't win against the person who just won't quit! After a while everyone will recognize, "Oh, she's serious, let me see what see is talking about."

Say this with me "*Persistence takes us from overlooked to overbooked!*"

Provide a three-person audience immense value the same way you would if it were a 3000+ audience

When I shared earlier that only three non-related guests would show up for my events, I was not limiting that attendee count to live local events, I meant virtual webinars too! Talk about being the mayor of virtual ghost land. That was me! It didn't matter. I knew that low turnouts were simply part of the process. You have to serve the three people that show up for you with high regard, tenacity and appreciation. By doing so, your brand will be fruitful and your numbers WILL multiply. You can apply this principle to blog posts comments, webinars, and frankly anything else.

Serve with a grateful spirit, it will take you far!

Get in the Mix

People crave intimate interaction. Yes, you might be a great writer. Yes, your social media posts are witty. BUT there _has_ to be MORE. What are you willing to do in order to truly make your brand sticky? Sticky as in you leave your audience with a lasting impression. Sticky as in they feel as if they know you. Sticky as in when they need help in your respective niche >>**YOU**<< are **THE** person to contact.

Blogging and social media alone won't do this. You need to get in the mix and go the extra mile in terms of interaction. There's something magical about hearing the human voice. It's the ultimate connector. Webinars, teleseminars and podcasting *(I call these high engagement activities)* are great ways for people to get a true sense of your personality and feel connected to you. Look at any of the personal brands that you admire most and I guarantee they are performing a combination of these activities.

21

Three Ways to Position Your Brand for Profits

"If you want it and expect it, it will be yours very soon."
— Esther Hicks

In this day and age, entrepreneurs strive to create something that will not only sell, but also will leave a mark on their audiences' minds. It is of utmost importance for growing companies to make sure that all their activities are focused on achieving a specific, targeted goal of positioning themselves so that they become unforgettable in the minds of their audiences. The best brands all have this in common: they have positioned themselves in such a way that they have stood out in the sea of competition.

In order to position your brand for profits, you need to remember a few things to make you stand out from the crowd:

Make your brand powerfully visible

Leverage social media for wealth generation. In the past you may have only utilized social media for communicating personally with family and friends, but now it's time for you to use it to grow your business like wildfire. Creating a powerful physical presence is very important in positioning yourself to receive profits. You have to make sure that everything people see on your brand – whether it is your physical appearance, or your website, your business cards, your brochure and marketing materials – they all point to the same message that you are trying to get across. Being consistent in how you tie up how you look with the quality of what you do is critical in creating an unforgettable brand.

Present yourself as the undisputed expert in your field.

You have heard this all too many times: that you need to position yourself as an expert in order to attract the clients that you love. Practically speaking, this means that you need to get clear on the value of what you are providing to your audience and have a compelling reason for them to continue following you and eventually buying from you. You need to be able to deliver your value in a simple, easy to understand way that captures the interest of your audience and keeps them coming back for more from you.

Create an impression that lasts

The saying "first impressions last" could not be more true and more powerful than in marketing. If you have not yet caught the attention of your clients, then you need to think over (very carefully) how you are doing things for your business. Get into the emotions of your audience. Emotions play a huge part in creating a brand that leaves a mark on people. To do this, you will need to know what people love about or what people don't like about your brand. These testimonials not only serve as your gauge of how your brand is doing, but also can be used as tools to let people know about your expertise and your authenticity.

You need to turn everything you do into an expression of how you want your audience to see you and you can create something special. This takes courage; to actively position your brand means you have to stand for something. Only then are you truly on your way to owning your very own position in the mind of your customer and generate more profits for your business.

22

How to Package Your Expertise

"You can get to where you want to be from wherever you are—but you must stop spending so much time noticing and talking about what you do not like about where you are."

— Esther Hicks

Packaging your expertise. I love this subject because it's touchy. It's a topic that some people embrace, but some women tend to shrink back from. The whole expert industry is a topic that makes some people roll their eyes. Here's the thing: the expert industry is so hot because there's money in it.

When you think about doctors, they make the amount of money that they make because they are experts. Now, let's take that a step further to doctors who are specialized in a particular area. They make even more money. When you think of a general physician compared to a cardiologist or an endocrinologist, the doctors with the specialties make more money. This is the same across the board in the expert industry. The reason that you want to package yourself as an expert is that the level of expertise that you can project and your positioning yourself as an expert will impact the amount of money that you are able to create. It's going to impact the type of opportunities that you attract. It's going to impact the level of transformation that you can create for the people that you work with.

People want to work with the best of the best. When you can package your expertise to show that you are a solid, renown expert, people are more likely to do whatever it is that you've taught them because a lot of times when you are a purpose-driven entrepreneur, it's not just about the money. It's not about people buying your products or services. It's about the people actually taking the steps and doing the things that you've taught them to do so that they can experience the transformation in their life that your package or your service has promised that they'll experience.

If you have not positioned yourself as an expert, it's hard for people to actually implement what it is that you've taught them. That's why it's important that you charge for your services because people don't necessarily act on free information. You will get some people who understand the value of whatever it is you're teaching them for free and they're going to act on it, but for the masses, there is something in the human psyche that leads most of us not to take action if there is not any skin in the game.

A lot of people just are not willing to do the work unless you are charging for it and unless you have positioned yourself as an expert. Maybe you're thinking that you are not an expert at anything. I disagree with you. I'd like to argue with you on that. You are an expert.

What comes to you naturally? This is an area where you could be an expert. What is it that you've been doing on your job? If you've been on your job for several years, maybe a decade or two, then you're an expert in whatever it is that you're doing in your place of employment. Or it may not be that you're going to be an expert in the exact thing that you do on the job because maybe that has run its course. Maybe you've done that long enough and you're ready to experience something different.

However, there are a ton of skills that you've cultivated while you've been on this career path and you can use those skills in your business. I'll take myself for example. I worked in IT quality assurance. I did a lot of performance testing, basically, which is simulating the human experience so that you can test how long response times are on servers, and how long different transactions take, etc. I have no desire to do that now. However, I am able to leverage my past experience with information systems in order to help people to create business systems for themselves because I love the business system piece of it. I am able to leverage that knowledge and that skill set from my employer. I'm not doing the same exact thing that I was doing with my employer, but I am able to leverage the best pieces of my employer as they are a great fit with my personality. I've been able to build a business around it.

If you're someone who is sick of what you were doing on your job, how can you take the skills that you used on your job and combine them with the skills and the creativity that brings you joy? How can you package all of that, bundle it up and make it into a business? Maybe you had to pay a lot of attention to detail. Maybe you planned events or you facilitated meetings. Maybe you wrote up agreements or contracts. How can you take these different pieces of your job and merge them with what fuels you and fires you up? Because you do not want to create another job for yourself. You want to create a business that you are passionate about. How can you combine those pieces to create the business that you want for yourself? That's your level, your area of expertise.

I see a lot of people on the sidelines who knock the expert industry. They roll their eyes and say things like, "Oh, she wants to be a life coach. Who says she's equipped to be a life coach? Is her life together?" You're always going to have haters and critics like this. If that is something that has scared you to death about stepping into your power as an expert, then get over it. There are people like that. There are what we call trolls in the world; people who just look for the negativity and always want to talk about somebody.

There are people who are going to say, "What gives her the right? Who told her that she has the right to be a consultant? Who told her she has the right to be a life coach? Who told her she could help people with their relationships? Who told her that she could help people with their money or create wealth?" There are going to be people like that. Let's keep it real. That is not your concern. What they feel about you is none of your business.

The only thing you need to be worried about is how you can breathe life into your business and how you can position yourself as an expert so that you can attract and create the type of clients that you were sent here to serve and the customers that you were sent here to work with. The fastest way to do that is by being confident in yourself, knowing that you are enough. You're expert enough. I don't care at what level you are in your business. You could be brand new in your business. So what? You already have been banking on those skills for several years.

Just because you may be new as an entrepreneur and you may be new to your business, you're not brand new to the world. You already have been leveraging those skills. You already have a track record with the skills and the talents that you have. You're not brand new. You're expert enough. You don't have to be the very best in the beginning. You just have to get started. In order for you to serve someone, you only have to be a few steps ahead of them.

If you are a level five, you are equipped to teach someone who is a level two, a level three or a level one. You only have to be a few steps ahead of the person who you are helping. The only thing that is required of you is that you are able to provide value to someone and provide increase in their life. You provide increase by providing the value. Know that you are expert enough.

Let go of what people think of you. That is an imaginary jail cell that you need to be released from. It is none of your business what other people think of you because nine times out of ten, your ideas about what they're thinking are wrong.

I talked earlier about you being your own worst hater. We create all of these make-believe scenarios in our heads. We tell ourselves all of these make-believe impressions that people have of us. Nine times out of ten, they don't even feel as poorly about us as we feel about ourselves. What I'm urging you to do is be confident in yourself and your abilities. Speak power over yourself and don't worry about what other people think about you. Because trust me, they don't care what you think about them. When it comes to whatever goals they have, when it comes to putting bread on their table, they're not going to slow down their car or their ship because of what you think.

Why are you letting someone else who doesn't live under your roof, who is not related to you, who can't help you, why are you letting what these people, these imaginary figures think hold you back? Everything that you want to experience is on the other side of fear. It's time for you to step up as the expert that you are so that you can generate the expert level of revenue and income and the freedom that you were created to achieve.

If you want a coach that will help you to push past fear and help you reach into your greatness as an influential brand, I invite you to apply for a complimentary breakthrough session with me: _http://brandybutleronline/breakthrough_

23

How to Podcast Like a Rockstar

"You must find the place inside yourself where nothing is impossible."
— Deepak Chopra

After the arrival of my newborn daughter, I found myself slipping into postpartum depression. I knew that I wanted to be wildly successful with online marketing, but I didn't know how to structure that business, I just knew that I wanted to do something with online business. This added fuel to my frustration because since I didn't have a working model, I felt as if I was dreaming.

Luckily a friend of mine introduced me to the concept of podcasting. From there I began listening to podcast shows and found two shows that would forever shape the vision that I had for my online business: *Smart Passive Income* with Pat Flynn and *Internet Business Mastery* with Jason Van Orden and Jeremy Frandsen. Listening to these shows excited me and reinvigorated me because now I had some working examples that provided evidence that my dream could become a reality. From there I began to incorporate spiritual podcasts into my daily regimen as well. This helped me to work on my mindset. Each day on my work commute I would balance business podcasts with spiritual podcasts. After a while, my postpartum depression subsided and I regained my vibrancy.

★★★★

I tell anyone who wants to dominate their niche and gain authority in their niche, that podcasting is a strategy they should include in their marketing.

The Internet streets tend to get jammed and flooded daily by millions of ambitious content creators who are vying for attention daily. Some content creators seek the attention of brands while others seek the attention of potential customers. Adult ADD is on the rise and with an estimated 200 million blogs in existence as of 2015, building your personal brand online can seem futile and intimidating. So what's an upwardly mobile woman who is on a quest to build her empire to do? One word. Podcast.

In comparison to the 200 million blogs in existence, there are only about 200,000 active podcasts in existence. I would LOVE to say that this disparity means that having a podcast improves your chances of getting noticed online by 1000%, BUT I'm not in the business of selling lollipops and pipe dreams. However, I can say with certainty that having a podcast show increases your chances of standing out and getting noticed as an expert in your niche.

How to Podcast Like an Expert:
Identify Your Brand Message
Your brand message is the foundation from which all of your content should flow. What does your brand stand for? What is it that you want to teach the world? Have a deep understanding for your brand's message before you start recording your podcast episodes. Identify how your podcast episodes can correspond to your blog posts, videos, as well as any programs or services that you offer.

Set the Tone for Your Brand

Decide on the type of energy and confidence you want to bring to your audience. Do you want to come across as serious, warm or snarky? Not only will you convey this tone in your own personality, but in the branding elements of your podcast. You would be surprised by the amount of impact that your podcast intro and podcast cover can have on the tone of your show. Make sure that the tone of your show compliments how you want to be perceived.

Have a Good Microphone

In the world of computer programming the term GIGO is used often: Garbage In Garbage Out. There is only so much noise that can be removed in post audio editing. Therefore, It is very important that you do your best to ensure that you are recording quality audio from the beginning with limited interruptions (try not to podcast near the window so that you can avoid picking up cars, dogs, and lawnmowers in your audio). Having a quality microphone will help you to have a show that sounds professional and pristine. Quality podcast recording equipment doesn't have to cost a fortune. The ATR2100 and the Blue Yeti are two popular microphone models that can be found for less than $100.

Have a Desired Call to Action

True experts speak not only to be heard, but also in order to influence their audience into a desired state of action. What is it that you want to gain from people listening to your podcast? Do you want listeners to visit your website, sign up for your free eBook, or signup up for your latest program? Direct your audience to the action that you want them to take when they finish listening to your show.

Promote Like Beyoncé

Love her or hate her, Beyoncé is EVERYWHERE you look. Your podcast show should be, too! Make sure that you distribute your podcast feed to as many distribution channels as possible. iTunes, Stitcher Radio, Sound Cloud, and now Spotify are all great audio platforms to establish a presence. Promote your podcast with visually appealing graphics that promote your episode's topic or guest. Social media staples such as Twitter and Facebook are not the only places to promote your podcast. Incorporate innovative podcast promotion techniques with mediums like Instagram, Periscope, Clammr, and Pinterest in order to drive traffic to your show

Lastly, enjoy the process. The BEST way to podcast like an expert is to be confident, be yourself, and have FUN! So you want to pull out your own hair when listening to the sound of your own voice? If so, you are in good company. Most people dread hearing the sound of their own voice. Grant yourself a healthy dose of grace and patience as you start your new podcast show. You'll be surprised how much your vocal and interview skills will develop show after show.

Now go forth, be great, and podcast like an expert! For More Inspiration and Business Building Articles, Check Out My Site *http://brandybutleronline.com*

24

10 Easy Ways to Create Your Very Own $5K Months Online

"God is not preparing the Blessing for YOU, He is preparing YOU for the Blessing."

— TD Jakes

Six-figure earner is a very seductive goal that many bloggers, coaches and creative entrepreneurs lust and yearn over. Like it or not, stating that you have earned over six figures in your business holds a certain cache and prestige. Heck, simply whispering the term, *"six figures"* even sounds smooth and sexy (*go ahead and try it, mouth it out with me siiixxxx fiiiiggurrrrezzzz*). Depending on your local cost of living — you could really do a few thangz with a six figure income (*yes, thangz with a "z"*).

While reaching six figures is definitely an attainable goal that one should wholeheartedly pursue, I like to track milestones in the pursuit of larger goals. When you are trying to achieve a large goal, it is important to experience a series of wins. Small wins build the staircase to momentum and BIGGER wins! Most importantly, wins create confidence, and confidence is critical in business.

What would it mean to your business if you generated $5k per month? That would be an annual revenue of $60k. Not bad at all! Especially when you consider that the average small business owner with less than five years in business makes less than $50k (Payscale). Let's not forget salaried workers. The United States median household income was reported to be $53,657 in 2014 (Yahoo).

Before I give you the low down on 10 easy ways to create your very own $5K months online...

Let me be clear about the different revenue category methods that I am describing:

- **Products** can be described as a physical (tangible) or an intellectual (intangible) good.
- **Memberships** are described as anything that requires an automated payment plan. This could be for the use of a service or for access to knowledge and/or skills.
- A **Course** is product where you are teaching a skill or method.
- The term "**Program**" is used loosely to describe a course, a coaching arrangement, a consultant service, or workshop (virtual and local).
- A **VIP Day** is a one day coaching intensive where you spend 6 – 8 hours serving your client within a 1 day intensive instead of spreading out the teaching over a series of weeks.
- **Sponsorships, Sponsored Posts, and Affiliate Sales** are not discussed in the following scenarios because I wanted to focus on ideas that content producers and subject matter experts can directly control.

I also want to give you a quick primer on the Cashable Content Cycle. The Cashable Content Cycle is how to use your free content (blogs, videos and podcasts) to drive traffic, interest and anticipation in your cashable content, which would include all of the revenue category methods listed above. Visit my website at BrandyButlerOnline.com to grab an image of the Cashable Content Cycle to help you understand it visually.

Keeping all of this in mind, I've taken the time to illustrate 10 different ways to generate $5k in your lifestyle business. The first section is comprised of 8 single solution examples. Afterwards, I outline two different hybrid product approaches.

Single Product Solutions (Each Option Generates $5K Monthly)

- Sell (200) $25.00 products
- Sell (100) $50 Memberships
- Sell (20) $250 Course Seats
- Sell (5) $1000 Programs
- Sell (10) $500 Program
- Sell (2) VIP Days $2500
- Sell (1) $5K Coaching Package
- Sell (1) Done for You Consulting Package at $5000

Hybrid Approach Example #1 (Monthly)

- Sell (4) $250 Course Seats ($1000)
- Sell (4) $500 Packages ($2000)
- Sell (2) $1K Programs ($2000)

Hybrid Approach Example #2 (Monthly)

- Sell (4) $25 downloadable products ($100)
- Sell (30) $50 Memberships ($1500)
- Sell (2) $5K Clients who are on a 3 payment schedule of $1700 per month ($3400)

I feel that it is important to list both the single and hybrid solution approaches, because there are several schools of thought around income maximization. Some thought leaders tell you to focus on one thing and have that item generate the bulk of your revenue (hence, the single solution approach). Other experts will tell you to diversify and let the sum of your efforts compound together for your good (hybrid approaches).

Personally, I generate this type of revenue by utilizing the hybrid product approach. You'll have to test and tweak to find out which strategies work best for your situation. One thing that I know for sure, there is no one size fits all in business. However, the common success denominator in all of these approaches will be the amount of people you are able to connect and resonate with (via web traffic, face to face or telephone interaction). Keep in mind that the low priced products and services will require more web traffic in order to generate the level of impact that larger ticket prices make.

As you can see, generating your first $5K per month is not rocket science. With a little elbow grease and much focus, your next $5K month is well within in your reach.

$60k may not buy you that fancy new yacht, but it's certainly nothing to scoff at. For some people, $60K is more than their current annual salary. Imagine if you work a full time job and your side business brings in $60K *(I bet you can dream up plenty of new thangz you would be able to do!)*. What I find even juicier is that once you know how to create $5K per month, you'll be further equipped to EARN EVEN MORE afterwards.

I want to remind you that the key to making sustainable money online is by sharing your expertise and building an audience. Every successful woman needs a tribe; a group of people who you were sent here to serve and that are attracted to your unique style, personality, and what you do in the world. You want to be intentional about growing your social media and positioning yourself with content so that you can actually make money. It's nearly impossible to make money if you haven't built your platform of targeted followers and you have no one to sell to. This sounds like an easy notion, but it takes strategy, dedication and work. However, the possibilities for online sales and exposure are limitless.

Conclusion

"You have within you, right now, everything you need to deal with whatever the world can throw at you."

— Brian Tracy

Now that you've reached the end of the book, I hope that you have begun to put the steps in place to start making your dream of leaving your job and building a business a reality. Remember, I am not telling you to just go out and QUIT your job. However, I know what it's like to be fed up, wanting to throw in the towel and say "EFF IT, I QUIT!" Stay encouraged that everything that you need is inside of you and that your new reality doesn't have to be far away. If the desire was placed within you the law of polarity states that there is a way for you to attain that desire. For every problem there is a solution. The opposite of lack is abundance. No matter how big your dream is, I want you to know that as long as you are in alignment you will not fail. The only way to fail is to quit on your dreams.

If you have finished this book, it's likely that you are a woman who has been successful in her career and has already served several years in her field. Look back over all of your achievements and accomplishments up to this point. Reflect on various challenges that you have overcome. You are a victor and to reach the next level in your life you will need to maintain a champion's spirit. This is a mental game of overcoming yourself. If you tap into the mindset of victory and start showing up in life as you want to *BE*, even before evidence shows that your vision is manifesting, you'll find that before long you'll begin to experience different pieces of your dream.

There is an old adage that seeing is believing. It's quite the contrary, believing is SEEING. After all, the core word in believing is BE.

What if I'm not even clear? I don't even know what to see?

If you still have too many thoughts swirling around in your head and you aren't clear about what it is that you want to do next, I suggest you go back to the clarity exercises that I outlined earlier, primarily the meditating exercise. However, I don't want you to get stuck in a place of overthinking. Remember: progress is not perfection. If weeks and months go by and you still don't know exactly what to do, I suggest that you begin putting at least one of your ideas into action. Even if that action doesn't result in your permanent business or career transition, you will benefit from the lesson in the process. In the words of Albert Einstein, "Nothing Happens Until Something Moves."

Imperfect Action Creates Perfect Momentum

Take responsibility for where you are right now. You don't have to stay stuck unless you want to. There are an abundance of resources online and great books that give very specific details about how to build businesses or live the life of your dreams. You are the author of your story and you have authority over your life. If you don't like something, change it. Just make sure that you maintain a good attitude and display gratitude for your life as it stands now. It's said that gratitude is the highest vibration that one can have. Energy is everything and we live in a vibrational world. Your thoughts send out vibrations that reverberate in the world.

Think of it this way: What if you have two children and you love them both the same? There is nothing that you would do for one that you wouldn't do for the other. However every time you give your children a gift, one of them is easily pleased and goes out of her way to show you that she appreciates what you give her, no matter how big or small the gift. Meanwhile, the other child always finds a reason to complain and whine. Anytime you give her a gift, the thank you is always accompanied with a big BUT. Too big, too small, not enough.

Who would you delight in giving more to?

Whoever can be trusted with very little can also be trusted with much, and whoever is dishonest with very little will also be dishonest with much. — Luke 16:10

You can absolutely create the lifestyle that you desire. Between contract work, hosting workshops, coaching, consulting, affiliate sales, online courses and online product selling, the possibilities for generating revenue are endless. With a rock solid strategy, belief system and focused action you can create the momentum you need in order to grow your vision.

Be willing to invest yourself. Investing in yourself will give you far greater returns than throwing your money away on clothes, hair, nails and random things. If you invest in your business it will take care of you. Show up in your business the way you want to be so that you can train people to see your brand in the way that you want them to view it.

Don't just sit on the sidelines of life, step into the arena. You have no idea how life will unfold until you step into your NEXT. There will be little clues and flashes along the way that will indicate that you are headed in the right direction, but the whole path will never be laid out for you entirely. This is called the process. Your journey won't just be about what you acquire but who you become along the way.

You must win within in order to successfully quit.

Regardless of whether you like your job or not, show up each day with a spirit of excellence. You never know if you will cross paths as an entrepreneur with former coworkers

Think of your job as an investor. It will take resources for you to build your platform. Your employer gives you the opportunity to make money. The most intelligent way to quit is to start making money in your business first before you do. While you are still working, make sure you have smart strategies and great branding. Charge beyond what you are worth, you deserve all of the business that you receive.

You don't know what you don't know, and it's what you don't know that keeps you stuck.

Lastly, it is important to realize that there is a lot about being an entrepreneur that you don't know. I hope that this book has given you a start in being able to begin your journey, but sometimes the information can be overwhelming and have you feeling like you are stuck. You may need help to get unstuck, and that's where working with a coach becomes so important. You may be working as hard as you can with everything that you know, but it may be something that you don't know that could help take your business to the next level.

Understanding when it's time to get help is one of the most important things that you can do for yourself. If you want a proven system for creating an influential brand that attracts premium clients and opportunities, head over to *www.brandybutleronline.com* to schedule a complimentary breakthrough session with me, you can also look at the different programs that I offer female entrepreneurs. I can personally guide you with a proven framework that will help you to fast track your results and move you closer to the day when you can JUST QUIT!

"Test me in this," says the Lord Almighty, "and see if I will not throw open the floodgates of heaven and pour out so much blessing that there will not be room enough to store it."- Malachi 3:10

About Brandy

Brandy Butler is an Online Business Coach and Strategist who is passionate about the power of spreading positive messages. She helps her clients to MAGNIFY their messages and to gain momentum in their businesses. It is her personal mission to help spread more positive messages to the masses. She helps her clients to get their platform messages maximum exposure while allowing them to focus on their central business functions. Bottom line, she handles her clients' key online platform marketing elements which frees them up to focus on their personal genius.

Prior to launching her business, Brandy spent 15 years in IT Project Management and Quality Assurance. She holds an undergraduate degree in Computer Information Systems and a Master's of Business Administration. She is a loving wife, mother of two wild boys and one precious princess. Visit BrandyButlerOnline.com to find out more about Brandy and to schedule your free complimentary discovery session.

Are you ready to experience a breakthrough in your life & business?

"If you are a female entrepreneur who is struggling with creating an influential brand and wants to increase your visibility and profitability so that you can achieve a lifestyle of freedom, I can help you.

Apply for your complimentary breakthrough session at *http://brandybutleronline.com/breakthrough*

Getting Started Online Basics

Website URL – If you haven't done so already, you'll want to secure the web domain addresses for your personal name and any other brand names that you are interested in using for your business before someone else reserves THEM.

I highly suggest securing your domain name and monthly web hosting with Bluehost. They have the easiest web set up and excellent customer service.

You can learn more about setting up your web address and hosting at *http://brandybutleronline.com/bluehost*

Lead Generation – As an entrepreneur, you want to make sure that you are always growing your database of potential clients and customers. Having a landing page or a squeeze page where prospects submit their emailS in exchange for free value that you provide, such as a free offer (ebook, report, consultation) or coupon is a great way to grow your prospect database. My favorite tool for lead generation is Leadpages. You can also USE LeadPages as a temporary placeholder for your website until it gets up and running. You can learn more about lead generation at *http://brandybutleronline.com/leadpages*

Email Marketing – It's said that the money is in your email list. There is truth in this to some degree. If you are a female entrepreneur who desires prosperity, then having an email list is a requirement. You can't perform successful lead generation and relationship marketing without one. Social media posting has it's place, however email marketing is an activity that will get you paid. For new entrepreneurs, I suggest Get Response for email service. You can learn more about email marketing at *http://brandybutleronline.com/getresponse*

Easy Web Design – Your website will help or hinder your image online. I suggest working with a graphic designer in order to create a strong AND cohesive brand style. However, if you want to get started easily and perfect your brand style along the way, you can always get started with a pre-designed web theme. Pre-designed themes will allow you to have a professional look out of the box regardless OF WHETHER YOU HAVE a graphic designer or not. You can learn more about pre-designed web themes at *http://brandybutleronline.com/studiopress*

Membership Websites – Earlier in the book, I gave an example of how you could possiblY make $5000 per month by selling membership services. The greatest benefit of utilizing a paid membership model in your business is that membership programs generate automated residual monthly income for you. Many wealthy entrepreneurs use membership sites as a passive revenue stream. Optimize Press is an industry leader when it comes to membership site software. I also use Optimize Press and it helped me to generate my first $50K in business. You can learn more about membership sites at *http://brandybutleronline.com/optimizepress*

Business Cards – Every time you step out of the house, there is an opportunity for you to make money! Be prepared to SHOW UP and present yourself as a professional every time you meet a new person or someone inquires about your services. Say "NO" to flimsy cards. Leave a lasting impression by using creative designs and thick quality card stock business card. You can learn more about quality business cards at _http://brandybutleronline.com/moo_

Paid Affiliate Disclaimer – *The links that I have shared are paid affiliate links. I will receive a commission at no additional charge to you, should you decide to purchase any of the products listed above utilizing my links. However, I have personally used each and every product outlined and I would not suggest using any of the services provided if I did not hold the company in high regard.*

Suggested Readings for Expanding Your Mindset

Instinct – TD Jakes

The Secret – Rhonda Byrne

Think & Grow Rich – Napoleon Hill

Secrets of the Millionaire Mind – T Harv Erker

The Passion Test - Janet Bray Attwood & Chris Atwood

Real Money Answers for Every Woman – Patrice C. Washington

Ask & It Is Given – Jerry & Ester Hicks

The Millions Within – David Neagle

I Declare – Joel Osteen

Sell or Be Sold – Grant Cardone

No Matter What – Lisa Nichols

The Science of Getting Rich – Wallace Wattles

How to Influence People & Make Friends – Dale Carnegie

The Alchemist – Paulo Coelho

Are you ready to transition into full time entrepreneurship?

- Are you ready to walk in your gift and get paid for doing work that ignites your spirit?
- Are you tired of dreading the upcoming work day?
- Are you ready to create an influential brand that is sizzling hot?
- Are you ready to become your own boss?
- Are you ready to launch a business that creates consistency

If you answered "yes" to any of the questions above, my Cubicle Exodus program is perfect for you!

This program was designed for women who are committed to walking into their greatness as full-time entrepreneurs.

Learn more at http://cubicleexodus.com

Join my community of prosperous female entrepreneurs!

Connect, celebrate, and mastermind with other like-minded female entrepreneurs who are focused on living lives of purpose and abundance.

It takes a village to build a vision. Don't grow alone. Sign up to join my superstar community at _http://brandybutleronline.com/community_

Bonus Feature: Superstar Online Brand Training Notes

What this training will cover:
- What a Superstar Online Brand is
- Nailing your Core Message
- Monetizing Online
- Brand Success Systems
- WINNING at your Level

I. **What is a Brand?**

Brand/

noun

    i.   a type of product manufactured by a particular company under a particular name.

       "a new brand of detergent"

       synonyms: make, line, label, marque; More

    ii. a brand name.

       "the company will market computer software under its own brand"

       synonyms: make, line, label, marque; More

    iii. a particular identity or image regarded as an asset.

       "you can still invent your own career, be your own brand.

       "a particular kind of something

       "his incisive brand of intelligence"

1. You are an asset.
   - The skills that you have, the wisdom that you have and the value that you bring – you are an asset wherever you go and the work that you do in the marketplace.
   - The whole purpose of having a superstar online brand mindset is to help you to move into the mindset of where you are charging for your work and along with it, doing what is necessary to be competitive in the marketplace, and to gain the visibility you need to continue to grow your brand.
2. Your Brand is not limited to your website or logo.
   - A lot of times when we think about branding, we think about graphics, logo, website and what it looks like and that is not what it's all about.
3. Your brand is YOU
4. Your brand is Your Message
   - The message is the foundation of your brand.
   - If you don't truly have a message that is worthwhile and that has substance – you won't be able to properly monetize.
5. Your packaging and positioning
   - Packaging and positioning is important because the way your brand looks will impact how people view your brand, as well as the price that they pay you.

II. **Your Brand Style**

Your brand style is the essence of who you are as a person, as a human being.

Brand Style

- Personality Tests (Strengths Finders 2.0)
- The more you understand your personality in its true essence, the more you will give yourself permission to be yourself.
- You don't try to fit in the box; you want to be yourself.
- For some people, they need to be an amplified version of themselves so they can reach people more effectively, but not really change their core individual but just dig in deep, so you can exude what it is that makes You "you-nique".
- It is great to figure out your different strengths because you don't want to spend a lot of time trying to fill out your weaknesses – you want to drive in your strengths because that's how you gain momentum and that's how you can drive the fastest (by operating in your strengths)
- Always outsource your weaknesses.
- There are also other types of personality tests (Myers-Briggs, etc.)
- It is a different experience when taking the personality test as an entrepreneur, because a lot of times, when you take personality tests, you operate as a member of an organization, so it is different when you take a test as an entrepreneur.
- This is a great place to start when trying to figure out your brand style.

- Brand Archetypes
- Research the 12 brand archetypes and see which one best aligns with your personality.

There are different ways to represent your characteristics in your brand, and the more you can represent them in your brand, the more you are able to attract your ideal audience and your ideal clients.

Aesthetics

- This is now the graphics and design of your brand.
- You want to have a brand you can be proud of – you want your brand to be polished
- In order to be a superstar online brand, you want to play a bigger game.
- You want to immerse yourself in your brand and have people be able to feel you as it relates to your niche.

Experience

How do you make people feel?

What types of feelings do people have for you and your brand?

Do they feel like you are professional?

Do they feel like you are warm?

Do they feel like you are sarcastic?

What's the experience that you want people to have when they interact with your brand?

IRL – In Real Life

Virtual – Brand Style

III. **How to Craft Your Message**

In order to have a superstar brand, you need to craft your message. You need to take the time because your message is the foundation for everything.

- You cannot properly monetize without a message.

1. Start with Why
   - What is your why?
   - What keeps you up at night?
   - What is it that keeps you going?
   - What is it that makes you never want to quit?
   - What drives you?
   - Why are your in business?

Your why should be bigger than taking care of your family – your why should be so big that it impacts your society, it impacts the world,

2. Select Your Niche
   - If you are someone who is new in the business, you need to select your niche – what niche is your business going to operate in?
   - Don't try to be everything to everyone.
   - Scale down and select what it is that you want to do.
   - Once you get one thing going on really well, then you can move on to doing something else.
   - First you need to focus – there are so many moving pieces that you need to be laser-focused.

How do you select your niche?

   a. Search on Google – look at some of the niche that you are interested in.
   b. Go into Amazon and search for books for the different keywords for your niche – see how well those books are performing, etc. The reason you are

doing this is because you want to strike where gold has already been found.

    c. Go and see what other people are doing and what is working for them. – don't copy anyone, but if a particular business model is working, there is no reason why it couldn't work for you.

3. Nail Your Message
   - Have Clarity
   - Be Confident
   - Clarity + Confidence = Ca$h

4. Multi-passionates: focus on birthing one thing at a time.
   - For most people, we do best at one thing at a time.
   - Focus on one thing, be successful on that and then build on other things.
   - Don't focus on making money, because the money is going to come. You need to focus on the WHY because it is the WHY that will keep you up on those days that you want to quit.
   - There are going to be days when you want to quit.
   - There will be days when you don't want to do it anymore or there will be days where you will think that everybody's doing it and it will no longer work for you. All of these different fears and pressure points are going to surface because you are human. That is why it is important that you love what you have built out.
   - Don't focus on the money because the money will not be enough to keep on going. Focus on the why.
   - If you can do that, it will align you to your purpose and that will keep you going.

Great Read: Start with Why by Simon Sinek

IV. **Monetizing online**

1. Internet Revenue Streams

   Physical products
   - If you are someone who sells physical products, having an online presence is a great way for you to gain income in addition to your local business area.
   - When you cover the internet, blogs and social media with your physical products, you will get some serious numbers.
   - People love physical products – they love items that they can touch and feel.
   - Great thing about physical products is that it allows you to get social proof. It is a great way to engage the audience and it gives you industry credibility.
   - Services
   - Consulting
   - Whatever type of work you do for someone.
   - Coaching
   - Freelancing, etc.
   - If you would like to earn extra income by monetizing your skills like writing, etc.
   - You can sign up for an account with freelancing sites such as oDesk.com (Upwork.com) or Elance.com
   - The higher quality of work you do, the more testimonials that you get, and the easier you can get into other freelancing positions.
   - There are also freelancing jobs in major publications.
   - Informational products
   - More and more people want to learn and people want to invest in that knowledge.
   - People love to improve themselves.

- You need to keep your products up to date.
- Examples:
- Books
- Downloads
- Courses
- Membership sites
- Affiliate marketing/joint venture partnerships
- Affiliate marketing is essentially getting commission for products or services you believe in, whether you have testimonials or have used the products yourself, etc.
- You are providing value when telling people about your affiliate's product or services.
- Participate in an affiliate marketing program that you have an experience firsthand.
- If you happen to not have experience on an affiliate brand, you should do your research on it and you should be at a place where you truly believe in it.
- Stay in integrity and maintain your credibility.
- For some people, affiliate marketing is just extra income, but some have made affiliate marketing a source of their passive income.
- Joint venture partnerships – are very similar to affiliate marketing.
- This is more of speaking for someone as an individual
- Maybe a new book, new course
- This is where you speak on behalf of that product or service.
- Any joint venture partnership should be with someone you actually believe in and trust – someone who is credible, who has integrity, and someone whom you do not feel that will negatively impact

your brand.
- Great way to gain credibility thorough someone else's email list.

6. Sponsored model (work with brands)
   - This is working with brands. It is you going directly to brands telling them how you and your event, podcast, etc., Can promote their brand and how you can gain them exposure.
   - You can also work on a network who has sponsorships offered.

7. Blogger networks
   - This is a great way to monetize your blogs
   - Having your own products and services allows you to have better income streams because it is something you can control.
   - You can control when your products launch
   - You can control if you want to create a podcast or a book
   - You can control if you want to create a membership club
   - You control when you are going to market these products or services.

Having your own products or services gives you a certain amount of power that even if you are making money with your affiliate or JV partner.

Choosing your revenue stream can depend on:
   - The why of your business
   - How much content you can send out.

V. **Werk Your Website**

1. Secure your domain name and hosting

    - You are in an industry where domains are constantly being bought and sold.
    - The moment that you get an idea, go ahead and secure your domain name so it will not be taken.

2. Use self-hosted Wordpress as your content marketing platform

    - Some people will not agree with me, but I think that it is important that you keep a self-hosted Wordpress as your content marketing platform.
    - You want to use Wordpress because it is user friendly, and most of the new companies build plugins and added functions for Wordpress sites.
    - It is very easy to have a Wordpress site.
    - If this is your business and you would like to build your revenue streams, do not build your website on a free platform.

3. Either find a web developer or take a DIY method and use classy pre-designed themes from StudioPress or ThemeForest.

    - The optimum and ideal solution is the web developer, but if you have a tight budget, you can use the DIY method, but if you go DIY, you need to use a classy and professional design.
    - No matter what your income level is, you can get it done, and you can get it done in style.

4. Be personable on your about page, don't make it sound like a resume. This will help you to immediately resonate with visitors.

    - People are tired of the corporate, straight from the box descriptions – they want color and they want it vibrant.

They want whatever it is that makes You you.

- Think about it as a story – how can you share the essence of you.

- Share who you are and bridge that with your skill set.

- You want to show your authority but you want to do it in a way that is personal.

- Take some time when you craft your About page.

- The message needs to shine on your about page.

- Use a FREE opt-in offer to grow your email list.

- You don't just want people to visit your site, because 90% of the people that visit your site are not going to come back.

- You get people to come back by grabbing their email addresses and keeping in contact with them through email and sharing your

- Blogposts in messages.

- Give people value – if you sell physical products, you can give out coupons.

- The money is in the list.

- You need to have a mixture of nurture emails and sales emails.

- Capture leads using landing pages – Leadpages or Optimize Press.

- The purpose of the landing page is for people to gain your free offer and in return, they give you their email.

- The landing page keeps your prospects focused.

Visibility.

- "You have to be seen + heard in order to get paid"

- Visibility is so key in having a superstar online brand.

- How do you gain visibility for your business?

- You need to make a connection with people who don't know you.

- Social media – connections and engagement

- You can target the exact people you want to do business with in terms of demographics, age, etc.

- Social media is about connections.

- You want to use your social media in such a way that you are connecting with people, and along with connecting with people, you are engaging them where they are.

- The more that you can get people engaged, the more they like you and the more they will buy from you.

- Blog – Inbound marketing and traffic

- You want to make sure that you have a blog.

- Having the blog gives you the ability to create free traffic for your website.

- Make sure you have a blog strategy in place.

- If you're someone that is new, you have to blog so people will know who you are.

- Podcast – Authority and expertise.

- Is a more advanced visibility technique, but this is a highly recommended technique.

- Podcasts allow you to have more following because people can hear you and your personality vs. just reading your blog posts.

- Having a podcast show allows you to be an authority in your space.

- Publish a book – Authority and credibility.
- Having a book automatically provides you credibility and authority.
- Great way to create initial revenue.
- You can sell your book either from the stage or off the stage.
- Public speaking – Authority, exposure, call to action.
- When you publicly speak, not only can you make money as a speaker but you can also send people to your website or get a sales call from them.

Relationship Systems

- You want your audience to feel that they really know you.
- You want them to feel like you are the only choice when the time comes for them to purchase your product or service.
- The way to do this is by your nurturing systems:
- Email marketing
- Make sure you are emailing them on a regular basis.
- Provide them with high value content.
- Make sure you are enriching their lives.
- Let your audienIn-person networking
- It makes your brand sticky to the people you meet in person
- Conferences, business events.
- Show up fully at the events you attend – show them your best self, so you can tell people what it is you offer with confidence so you can have a follow-up conversation after.
- Free consultations or discovery calls
- Free consultations are not a waste of your time
- If you don't convert the prospect, you will have an idea of what conversations are going on in the marketplace.

- Always look at consultations and discovery calls as an opportunity for yourself – a way to get more clients or a way to get market insight.

- A free consultation can also be a way for you to look into people's behaviors so you can better create products and services for your ideal clients.

- If you can provide value in your free consultation, most likely the prospect will not hesitate to get back with you because the service you provided them was authentic and the solution you gave was the best solution for their problem.

- Not all free consultations convert on the spot – they may convert later, sometimes, they may not convert at all. Just make sure that when you do your consultation, you don't give them skimpy value. Be sure that you provide people value and knowledge that they could easily implement with their businesses, careers and their life.

- Show up as the best version of yourself and give the solution that you think would help your client or prospect get to the next level of the problem they are facing.

- If you don't skimp on the information you give, your discovery calls will convert at a much higher rate.

- Give real solutions!

- Webinars, teleseminars and Google Hangouts

- These are phenomenal relationship systems because for one, people love live events.

- People get a chance to hear your voice, your personality, and they can decide instantly whether they like you or not.

- Live events are great ways to build your tribe. You need a tribe of people who are buzzing about your products and services. You need people celebrating you and that is the purpose of the tribe. They are there for you, will show up for you and will cheer you on no matter what.

Sales Systems

- You got to have sales to keep your dream and passion going!

- Most people who have jobs are used to having deliverables and tasks that you are responsible for and you have a timeline to fulfill these tasks so the notion of sales is totally different. For some people, this is a tough pill to swallow and it is sometimes hard to transition into this mindset.

- So many people are talking about brands but keep the sales conversation in the low.

- Sales conversations are important and should never be ignored.

- Sales funnel – begins with discovery (the top of the funnel) and continues through low-cost products and services, right down to your high-end programs and services.

- You need to grow your email list as it is the start of your funnel

- If you are not growing your email list, you are missing the opportunity to sell your products and services.

- Have multiple streams of income that you build online so you can have a viable business – you can't eat passion.

- Special offers and coupons

- Coupons are more for people who have physical products.

- If you have an informational product or service, you can provide special offers.

- Have a time frame for your special offers

- Make sure that whatever your offer is, it has to be in alignment with the way you position yourself and the way you market yourself.

- You don't want to package yourself too cheap – but this is a unique case by case basis.

- Calling for cash

- You have to call for cash.

- You have to follow-up with prospects.

- Follow-up with people who are not yet your prospects, but you feel that your products and services can provide value for them.

- You have to go after the cash – you should ideally be spending at least an hour a day where you call for cash, following up with prospects and leads.

- It is not just about creating an online presence – you have to let people know what you have to offer. Go out and get the sale!

- Sales processing – eCommerce

- If you are somebody who is new to getting sales, you have to have an eCommerce setup to capture and document your sales.

- You can also have a merchant account where you can process payments over the phone.

- Great reads:

- To Sell is Human – Daniel Pink

- Launch – Jeff Walker

- 10X – Grant Cardone

Assess Where You Are

- Bootstrap Startup

- Limited finances

- Start where you are and eventually you will be able to invest in your business.

- Sometimes when you first start out as an entrepreneur, you don't even have limited finances. You just have a limited mindset about how much you are going to invest in your business.

- Maybe you don't believe in yourself enough.

- Creative resourcing

- If you can work out on your mindset, you can find it in yourself to invest more on your business.

- Do it yourself functions

- Never compromise professionalism due to bootstrap status. Invest as much as you can when you are working outside of your skillset.

- CEO Mindset

- This is not about "I can't afford this" mindset.

- This is a mindset coming from a place of abundance – you still understand your limitations but you start from the "I can't do this" to the "I can do this" mindset.

- Outsource tasks

- Outsourcing can be sometimes scary.

- Whatever it is that somebody can do better than you and can help take your brand to the next level, you need to outsource.

- If something is totally out of your skillset, have someone else do that for you. (For example: brand graphics)

- Be open to outsourcing – that way you don't overwhelm yourself and you don't stretch yourself too thin.

- Systems Upgrade

- You have to realize that you will come to a certain point where you need to upgrade your systems so that you will have the right analytic to support your business growth.

- Figure out how to effectively use your time on getting help and investing in your business because you can only get so far without help.

- Invest in Business Development

- When you want to grow your business to the next level, you have to also invest in developing your business.

- Coaching

- Get a mentor
- Courses
- Enroll yourself in a course so that you level up your learning to new trends and learnings.
- Mastermind
- Be in a group that is like-minded that can help you see things that you are blind to or do not see.
- Marketing Budget – 20%
- You need to put some money into your marketing.
- Studies show that you should be spending at least 20% of your revenue back into your marketing efforts (thus the 20% marketing budget).
- Includes paid traffic.
- The more you invest in the business, the greater the return you will get.

VI. **Win!**

Advanced Superstar Online Brand Strategies – How can you get brand visibility?

1. Write guest blog posts

    »   You can team up with a blogger and write guest articles on their blog.

    »   You have to team up with someone whose writing is compatible with your brand.

    »   Writing a guest post allows you to be exposed to greater audiences and it is a great way to build traffic for your website.

    »   Writing a guest blog post is great way for different publications to find out about you.

    »   A superstar brand is about you becoming a brand online that people Know, Like and Trust so that you can get paid.

2. Pitch yourself

    »   This is so critical for your brand.

    »   You snatch opportunities by pitching yourself and letting people know that you are worthy to be featured, you are worthy to be heard and you have a message that you need to deliver.

    »   Don't be self-defeating. Step outside of yourself for a minute, and take the challenge to pitch yourself!

    »   All it takes sometimes is for you to get into one media outlet and that is how you create a domino effect.

    »   If you want to build your superstar brand, being online is not enough. You have to get out into your backyard and start pitching yourself.

Places where you can pitch:

    a. News

    b. Conferences

3. Host your own events
   - » Hosting your own events builds your credibility.
   - » If your brand is credible, you build your authority and you position yourself as a leader.

4. Speak for free
   - » Start where you are. Pitch yourself, call for cash and call organizations and see if they are open about you speaking about your subject.
   - » Eventually, you will end up with paid speaking opportunities or you will land opportunities to pitch or sell your product to these organizations.

   Places you can speak for free:

    a. Elementary schools

    b. Colleges

    c. Community organizations

5. Collaborate with other Influencers
   - » You cannot build your business on your own – it takes a village.
   - » Start looking at other influencers on a peer level and not just a fan level.
   - » Start contacting these influencers so they can collaborate with you by guesting on your live event, teleseminar or webinar.
   - » This can help you build your network, which in turn, can build your authority in the business.
   - » Mix and mingle with other influencers and see what type of opportunities will come your way.
   - » Builds authority and exposure

6. Use premium images – Creative Market, Dollar Photo Club, PicMonkey, and Canva.

> » The images that you use for your brand really are a core feature of your packaging and the way people see you.
>
> » You cannot use bootleg, subpar graphics for yourself and your business and then try to charge premium prices – it is not in alignment.
>
> » Use premium images so that you can portray yourself and package yourself as a professional that commands a decent dollar price.
>
> » You cannot generate wealth without taking care of the way your brand is represented.
>
> » You need to use royalty free images.
>
> » If you have income, team up with a graphic designer, if you don't, use something like PicMonkey or Canva to edit your images.

Made in the USA
Lexington, KY
11 January 2017